Key management models

Key management models

The management tools and practices that will improve your business

Steven ten Have, Wouter ten Have, Frans Stevens and Marcel van der Elst, with Fiona Pol-Coyne

Prentice Hall

FINANCIAL TIMES

An imprint of **Pearson Education**

London ■ New York ■ Toronto ■ Sydney ■ Tokyo ■ Singapore ■ Hong Kong
Cape Town ■ Madrid ■ Paris ■ Amsterdam ■ Munich ■ Milan ■ Stockholm

PEARSON EDUCATION LIMITED

Edinburgh Gate
Harlow CM20 2JE
Tel: +44 (0)1279 623623
Fax: +44 (0)1279 431059
Website: www.pearsoned.co.uk

First published in Great Britain in 2003

© Pearson Education Limited 2003

The right of Stephen ten Have and Wouter ten Have to be identified as authors of this work
has been asserted by them in accordance with the Copyright, Designs and Patents Act 1988.

ISBN: 0 273 66201 5

British Library Cataloguing in Publication Data
A CIP catalogue record for this book can be obtained from the British Library.

This publication is designed to provide accurate and authoritative information in regard to
the subject matter covered. It is sold with the understanding that neither the author nor
the publisher is engaged in rendering legal, investing, or any other professional service. If
legal advice or other expert assistance is required, the service of a competent professional
person should be sought.

The publisher and contributors make no representation, express or implied, with regard to
the accuracy of the information contained in this book and cannot accept any responsibility
or liability for any errors or omissions that it may contain.

10 9

Typeset by Pantek Arts Ltd, Maidstone, Kent.
Printed and bound in Great Britain by Biddles Ltd, King's Lynn, Norfolk

The Publishers' policy is to use paper manufactured from sustainable forests.

Contents

The Management Models

About the authors

Steven ten Have

Steven ten Have read law and psychology at Utrecht University and earned a Master's Degree in Business Administration from Nijenrode University. At this moment he is the Vice-Chairman of the Board of Berenschot Group, a large independent consultancy firm based in The Netherlands. In 2002 he completed his PhD at Twente University. In his thesis he describes the change management practices of Nokia and ST Microelectronics and several other companies.

Wouter ten Have

Wouter ten Have read economics at the Vrije Universiteit, Amsterdam. He works at Berenschot and is the Managing Director of The Change Factory, a consulting group specializing in organizational change and strategy implementation. He is the author and co-author of several books and articles concerning strategy implementation, change management and leadership.

Frans Stevens

Professor Frans Stevens studied organizational sociology in Leiden, social psychology in Utrecht and economics in Rotterdam and Utrecht. After working as an industrial consultant for the Dutch government and as a manager at a steel and construction company for five years, he went to work for Philips International in 1974. Professor Stevens was appointed as EFQM Professor in Total Quality Management at the Ecole Européenne des Affaires in Paris. In this function, he teaches for this university in Paris, Oxford, Berlin and Madrid. From 1995 until 2000 he was the Managing Director of the INK (The Dutch Institute for Quality Management).

Marcel van der Elst

Marcel van der Elst obtained his graduate degree in industrial engineering and management at the Eindhoven University of Technology. He worked as a strategy consultant with Arthur D. Little and Berenschot. Marcel van der Elst is currently active as a senior consultant with Solving International in the USA.

Fiona Pol-Coyne

Fiona Pol-Coyne read Chinese language and culture and Korean at Leiden University in The Netherlands. Her studies included extended periods in both China and South Korea, at the Beijing Language Institute and the Hanguk University of Foreign Studies respectively. She later completed an MBA at the NIMBAS Graduate School of Management in Utrecht. In September 2000, she joined Berenschot as a strategy consultant.

Preface

In the world of management and organization, it is fortunately still ideas that really matter, and not models. Nonetheless, it seemed that a book on the most popular management models would certainly not be surplus to requirements. After all, managers and consultants spend considerable time discussing existing models and thinking up new ones, to say nothing of putting them into practice in their daily work. For them, models and theories offer not solutions to organizational problems, but rather ways to reduce the complexities and uncertainties involved – nothing more, but definitely nothing less.

The vast array of management models on offer is a source of bewilderment for many, managers and consultants alike. Attracted by the challenge of establishing some sense of order, we have drawn up an overview of some 50 of the most frequently used and cited management models. A brief description of each model is provided, together with suggestions as to its application. Comments have also been included and, where appropriate, attention is drawn to any potential limitations or shortcomings.

The collection of management models is largely the result of literary research. We arrived at the final selection by asking some 70 managers, consultants and academics around the world which models they consider to have been the most helpful in their own work. For this purpose, we defined a model as a tool that can be employed to enable or enhance the daily functioning of both organizations and the managers within them, or to solve related problems. The collection thus reflects those ideas and insights which have proven to offer solid footing, are considered workable in practice and have contributed positively towards solving the organizational problems with which managers and consultants are frequently confronted.

We would like to emphasize that the book is intended neither as a 'top 60' of popular management models, nor as a prescription for 'good' management and organization. Rather, the number, the variety and the differences between the models included in the collection aim to place in perspective not only each individual model but management models in general. Together with the descriptions and typifications of the various models, this reduces the danger that managers will be tempted to view the next popular model that happens to come along as a panacea for whatever ailments their organization happens to be suffering from at the time.

The majority of the models would not stand up to a high degree of scientific scrutiny, many being simply memory aids, useful ways of ordering reality. They offer a common language when it comes to solving problems, contain inspiring typifications, but above all are of great practical value when it comes to analysing situations and identifying possible courses of action. The criterion for inclusion, therefore, was not whether the models selected are scientifically or technically sound, but whether they actually work.

It is with both pleasure and pride that we present this collection. We are confident that the managers and consultants who use it will possess the requisite maturity, intelligence and discerning ability to place the models we have included in perspective, and not be tempted to consider 'trendy' models as a serious alternative to sound, creative, consistent management and advice. For each specific situation, they will subsequently be in a position to identify the underlying problem and determine how best to deal with it in that specific instance. Unfortunately, neither a single model nor a whole list of models can offer any guarantee that a manager or consultant will deal with an organizational problem objectively and to the best of his or her ability. Models can nonetheless offer valuable insights and a sound framework on the basis of which the right choices can be made – right from the point of view of the profession, the organization and also of the managers and other employees involved.

It was never our intention to produce an unambiguous taxonomy of models, based on a simplified overview of our field of work. Assuming that such a taxonomy already exists in the minds of good managers and consultants, our aim is rather to supplement it by providing additional ideas and insights, and sound, easily comprehensible descriptions of management models. Thus enriched, the taxonomy will enable managers and consultants to quickly determine which model is most appropriate for a given situation, while recognizing its limitations. This ties in neatly with our field of work, confronted as we are on a daily basis with the extreme difficulty of successfully managing, changing and providing contingent advice simultaneously. We view this book as a means not only give expression to this complexity, but also to make it somewhat less unmanageable.

It is impossible to thank personally all of those who have been involved in the publication of this book. There are nonetheless a few who deserve a special mention. First of all, we would like to extend our thanks to Professor Manfred Kets de Vries (INSEAD), who in an interview with Suzanne Weusten opened the door to his world of models and concepts, providing us with important insights into the mentality of the manager and the role of management models therein. Then there is Robert Kranenborg, inspired chef and co-owner of restaurant Vossius in Amsterdam, who guided us through his world of recipes and their uses.

By so doing, he made a valuable contribution towards not only appreciating models, but also being able to place them in perspective – like recipes, they form an important part of the profession, but cannot replace and must never be seen as a substitute for professional skill and expertise. For this our thanks. Joep Bolweg, our admired colleague and an absolute professional, played an important role in the discussion about the meaningfulness (or otherwise) of management models. His insights and other contributions have enriched the work immeasurably. Chris Fraass, friend and chef of restaurant 'De Burgemeester' Linschoten, inspired us to work further with the metaphor of management models and recipes. Behind the scenes, invaluable work was carried out by Michiel ten Raa and Erna van der Pauw – without their efforts, getting this book to publication would have been a very different story. Marieke de Wal, Tineke Boersma en Esther van Linge have done a lot of research. We like to thank them for their efforts and commitment. Then there are our driven co-authors, Marcel van der Elst and Fiona Pol-Coyne. Marcel was responsible for writing up many of the models included in the collection, in addition to which he played an important part in many of the substantive discussions. Fiona elaborated a number of models and carried out a critical review of the remainder. She also played a crucial role in finalizing the work in preparation for publication.

We wish the readers of this book as much pleasure, inspiration, and as many moments of reflection as we have experienced in its creation.

Steven ten Have
Wouter ten Have
Frans Stevens

Using the book

In this book a succinct description of the essence ('The big idea') and use-fulness ('How to use it') of each of the models is provided. In addition, we have included remarks ('The final anaylsis') on the limitations of each model and potential pitfalls with regard to their use. The description of each model is accompanied by one or more illustrations of a demonstrative nature. In addition, a number of models are supplemented by case studies describing how the model in question was used in a specific situation. Should you require more information on a specific management model, please refer to the list of References and further reading at the back of the book.

The models can be roughly categorized as 'Strategy', 'Organization', 'Primary process', 'Functional processes' (for instance, financial or commercial) and 'People and Behaviour'. The models are, however, not ordered according to their subject matter, but are in alphabetical order, with an icon representing the relevant categorization.

 Strategy

 Functional processes

 Organization

 People and behaviour

 Primary process

Introduction: management models and recipes – it's what you do with them that counts

O n the face of it, there appears to be little or no relationship between the occupation of chef and the daily activities carried out by a manager. Management is, after all, widely viewed as a 'thinking' profession, whereas chefs use not only their heads, but also their hands. Furthermore, while the fruits of a chef's creativity are both tangible and immediate, most managers must generally wait considerably longer. If, however, one compares the way in which managers use management models with the way in which chefs use recipes, parallels emerge. To establish just how chefs and the way in which they employ recipes can act as an example to managers with regard to the use of management models, we visited Robert Kranenborg.

Kranenborg is the chef and owner of the Vossius in Amsterdam. He gained experience at L'Oustau de Baumanière in Les Baux de Provence and Le Grand Vefour in Paris, and among other places, was a chef at La Cravache d'Or in Brussels, the Corona in The Hague and the Amstel Hotel in Amsterdam. In 2001 he opened his own restaurant, specializing in shellfish, game and fowl.

Kranenborg is a phenomenon in the Dutch culinary scene. It is thanks to him that La Rive (the restaurant in the Amstel Hotel in Amsterdam) was awarded its second Michelin star. Despite this achievement, Kranenborg came to the conclusion that his desire to excel as a chef would be better served by opening his own restaurant. Together with his business partner, John Vincke, he subsequently did just this: Vossius in Amsterdam was born.

A conversation with Kranenborg reveals a man who, even after 30 years, is full of passion for his vocation. Why does someone choose to become a chef? 'You must want to work with your hands, to create something from which another will derive pleasure; you must be vain enough to really want to give something of yourself.' As a chef, you are, in effect, an intermediary, linking producers, who are proud of what they have to offer, and guests.

It goes without saying that a chef must also truly enjoy good food. For Kranenborg, the key words are craftsmanship and pleasure – pleasure in the nature of the work itself, but also in the independence it can bring with it.

Can a profession offering so much satisfaction and pleasure be learned? According to Kranenborg, yes, but the speed of development naturally depends on the degree of talent. 'Natural talents aren't afraid of taking risks or changing: to really get somewhere in this profession you have to be prepared to unleash your own potential.' Developing yourself in this case means investing in a thorough culinary education: working under different masters, for different types of guests, in different types of restaurants. The wonderful thing about learning in this way is that, having become familiar with all the products, methods and techniques available, you can carry on experimenting with combinations forever.

The same applies to those managers who really understand the essence of models and have had a chance to put them into practice in a variety of situations: they can shake off the constraints without losing sight of the basic premise. They are capable of judging whether a particular model is appropriate for a given set of circumstances and applying it without making the application a goal in itself. Or as Kranenborg puts it, the better your education and the more insight you have into your own style, the longer you can go on developing yourself as a chef. You omit certain things, you let yourself be inspired by specific products and creations of others – but what you never ever do is work completely by the book.

According to Kranenborg, there's not much left to discover: 'Everything's already been invented'. Rather, it's all about combining things, about lending your own style to a dish, developing new combinations based on what you've learned. 'You have to be able to translate what it is that your customers want and have an excellent sense of taste and texture yourself, which you have to be constantly developing and trying out.' This does not mean simply following the current trend, though.

This goes for managers too: while you are not expected to think up any new models, you have to understand the likely consequence of applying the existing ones, i.e. predict how the result will 'taste'. Just as for a chef, the combination of previous experience and talent can help the manager to make small adjustments to standard models, thereby creating a tailor-made solution for the organization.

For a chef, self-development means daily self-evaluation. Evaluation on the basis of feedback from the customer ('empty plates'), as well as from colleagues and masters. This entails keeping a step ahead of your colleagues but also being open about your own methods. Developing a new dish can sometimes take up to three months: tenacious as he is, Kranenborg keeps at it until it is absolutely perfect. He admits that, in spite of his experience and technical skill, he is sometimes surprised by the results. 'What is essential is that you know where and when to intervene. You really have to understand what the basic components are, as well as the potential effect of the various ingredients on each other.'

Here, too, one can see a similarity with how organizations work. Even if a model is technically appropriate, it may not lead to the desired result when applied within a specific organization. In such a case, the model does not necessarily have to be rejected; rather, it is up to the manager to understand the situation, to make the adjustments necessary to bring the organization back on track, and to subsequently achieve the original aim.

Just as a chef has to work on a dish until it is perfect, so must a manager constantly work on his or her organization. Provided that you have the courage to act on your own convictions, it is foolish to change course at the first sign that things are not going as you intended. As with cooking, it is all about the combination of inspiration and transpiration: inspiration refers to making a choice and staying focused, transpiration to working in a consistent fashion and ensuring that you evaluate sufficiently.

Whilst once more emphasizing the importance of remembering your education, the basis of your profession, Kranenborg points out that certain recipes are obsolete. Some classical dishes, for example, are simply too heavy for today's tastes. But you will always use the techniques you have learned, ultimately supplemented by new ones of your own. In other words, you are constantly gaining insight. New techniques enable you to carry out your profession better than ever. Being open to new techniques and ideas is important not only for your own self-development, but also for the development of the profession.

The talent of the chef is, of course, important, but ultimately it is the team as a whole that determines the quality of what comes out of the kitchen. 'The concept as a whole must work', as Kranenborg puts it. He is very much results-oriented, and attaches great importance to the development of the individuals on his team. This in turn calls for the evaluation of individual performance. 'I want to see how people work, to see if they have the requisite feeling and finesse.' He is happy to leave interviews and the like to others. 'I'm not so concerned about someone's character, it's what they can do that interests me. A "nice" team is not going to get you very far.' According to Kranenborg, temperament inevitably comes with talent and you simply have to be able to manage it.

As a coach, he derives great satisfaction from tracking the development of his charges. Being able to let go, to not want to do everything yourself, is one of the hardest things for a chef, as it is for many managers. It is nonetheless Kranenborg's level that serves as the standard that both colleagues and dishes have to match up to. Everyone knows this – and they know when they're not up to scratch. Kranenborg: 'I never have to fire someone – you either fit in or you don't'. But this doesn't mean that someone who at his/her own request has been given a position for which he or she was not yet ready is a failure. 'It would be arrogant not to offer them anything – everyone needs time to develop. In a professional organization you should be able to take a step back and try a new approach.' This is something that Kranenborg makes very clear to his team, and he and his colleagues are often pleasantly surprised by what people who do just this are ultimately able to achieve.

To the final question of whether recipes can be 'good' or 'bad', Kranenborg answers: 'there is no such thing as a bad recipe'. Neither are there any criteria to determine what constitutes a good recipe, though as a chef you have the right to be of the opinion that a certain combination doesn't work. The most important thing is to try and be original and to cook in a way that suits you. Guests must always be able to criticize the combinations you present, as this is to do with your style, but they should never be able to fault you on your knowledge of products, techniques and methods: 'I want to be able to look every guest straight in the eye'. Kranenborg's aim is to provide the best he can for his clientele, while constantly striving to attain higher levels of perfection himself.

Not everyone has to have blind faith in every model – but if they work for managers and for organizations, then they are useful tools. However, as Kranenborg says, 'we're not circus performers'. In other words, models should not be used purely for their own sake. A model is and remains a tool which, when combined with knowledge and experience, and employed at the right time, can help an organization find solutions to certain problems.

The management models

Activity-based costing

The big idea

Traditional cost accounting models allocate indirect costs (overhead) on the basis of volume. As a result, the costs of high-volume products tend to be overrated, while the costs of low-volume products are underrated. Contrary to traditional cost accounting methods, *activity-based costing* (ABC) calculates the 'true' costs of products, customers or services by attributing indirect costs based not on volume, but on required or performed activities.

The underlying assumption of ABC is that it is not the products or customers themselves, but the activities carried out to respectively make or serve them that cause costs. As different products require different activities, each using a different amount of resources, the allocation of costs should be weighted accordingly.

When making business decisions, knowledge of true costs can help to:

- establish economic break-even points;
- identify 'profit-makers' and 'losers' (i.e. assess 'customer value');
- highlight opportunities for improvement;
- compare investment alternatives.

ABC costing has been responsible for many infamous 80/20 graphs and bar charts presented by managers and consultants, outlining products, customers, channels and services that actually lose money for the company!

When to use it

There are five steps in performing a simple ABC analysis:

1. Define cost objects, indirect activities and resources used for the indirect activities.
2. Determine costs per indirect activity.
3. Identify cost drivers for each resource.
4. Calculate total indirect product costs for the cost object type.
5. Divide total costs by quantity for indirect cost per individual cost object.

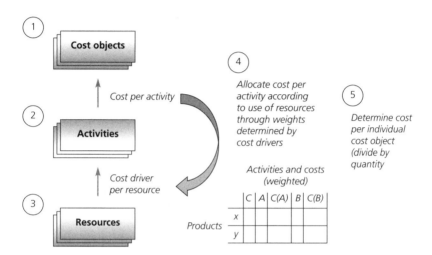

Cost objects are products, customers, services or anything else that is the object of the cost-accounting endeavour. *Activities* could be anything a company does to do its business: receiving, loading, packing, handling, calling, explaining, selling, buying, promoting, calculating/computing, writing orders, reading orders, etc. *Indirect activities* are not directly attributable to cost objects. *Resources* are machines, computers, people, or any other capacity or asset that can be (partly) allocated to an activity.

The final analysis

ABC enables segmentation based on true profitability and helps determine customer value more accurately. As such, it is the first step toward *activity-based management* (ABM).

ABC does not assess efficiency or productivity of activities, even though this may be highly important for improvements. Also, ABC assumes that it is possible to uniquely identify cost objects, activities and resources. At the end of the day, the outcome of an ABC analysis is only ever as accurate as its input.

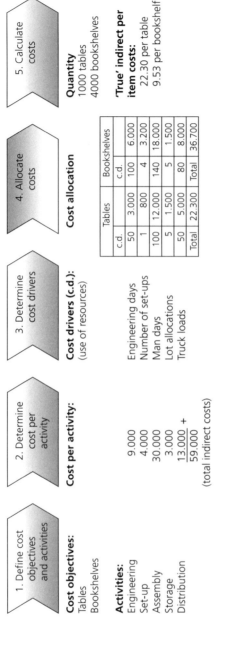

| 1. Define cost objectives and activities | 2. Determine cost per activity | 3. Determine cost drivers | 4. Allocate costs | 5. Calculate costs |

Cost objectives:
Tables
Bookshelves

Cost per activity:

Activities:

Engineering	9.000
Set-up	4.000
Assembly	30.000
Storage	3.000
Distribution	13.000 +
	59.000

(total indirect costs)

Cost drivers (c.d.):
(use of resources)

Engineering days
Number of set-ups
Man days
Lot allocations
Truck loads

Cost allocation

	Tables		Bookshelves	
	c.d.		c.d.	
	50	3.000	100	6.000
	1	800	4	3.200
	100	12.000	140	18.000
	5	1.500	5	1.500
	50	5.000	80	8.000
	Total	22.300	Total	36.700

Quantity
1000 tables
4000 bookshelves

'True' indirect per item costs:
22.30 per table
9.53 per bookshelf

In this simple example, a company has identified five activies required to make both of its products: tables and bookshelves. The resources used in these activities would traditionally be allocated based on item volumes. The indirect costs would thus be: 59.000 / 5000 = 11.80 per table and bookshelf.

Although the same activities are used for both products, management feels that the resources are utilized more by tables than bookshelves. Using ABC proves management to be correct, demonstrating that each table cost more than twice as much to produce as each bookshelf.

Adizes' PAEI management roles

The big idea

No individual manager can meet all the demands of his or her internal and external environment. For effective management, an organization ought to bring together a team of leaders that – when working together in harmony – can scale the most complex and dynamic of issues.

According to Adizes (1979), the four key elements that make up a successful management team can be translated into four management roles:

- the producer (P)
- the administrator (A)
- the entrepreneur (E)
- the integrator (I).

There is no 'one for one' role manager: each manager brings to the table a mix of management styles and characteristics. Consequently, a team may consist of fewer or more individuals than four. Essentially, management's success is dependent on the extent to which these roles are fulfiled.

The relative and absolute importance of each role is determined by situational factors, such as the organization type, its size, its external environment and its stage of development. This last is important, as each stage of development requires different management accents, i.e. a greater degree of entrepreneurialism in the early stages, as opposed to a more administrative and integrative focus later on.

When to use it

The model can be used not only to bring the right people together, but also to encourage people with different styles to work together effectively.

Characteristic	Producer	Administrator	Entrepreneur	Integrator
Work habits	Long hours, restless, serious, little emotion, 'do-it-now', get it done, 'hard work solves all problems', always fighting deadlines, explains by doing, feels that teamwork is less efficient due to communication needs	Neat, organized, low key, control-freak, careful, step-by-step, adhering to rules and procedures, punctual, schedules meeting as a rule, rather than for reason, seeks standardization, thinks teams work if they follow team roles	Irregular hours, may at times not show up at all, playful, jokes, tells stories, talks, inspires, dreams, exaggerates, doesn't wait, action-orientated, hopping around, unexpected views, teams are an audience for the entrepreneur's vision	Reliable, trustworthy, warm, caring, good listener, always there, seeks compromise, tries to understand people, empathic, solves problems by talking them through, sees team work as a goal in itself
Visual appearance	Conservative	Conforms to standard	Trendy, retro or artsy	Warm, accommodating
Likes you if you...	get things done	follow the rules	follow directions, play into his/her thought process	get along with others, confide in him/her, give him/her inside information
Dangerous when you...	are not working (hard enough)	want to change things	lack initiative or do things without his/her consent	criticize people in public, speak your opinion on behalf of others
Opinion of/attitude towards:				
Producer	'Everybody should be like this'	'It won't work like this in the long term'	'Useful'	Tries to turn the producer's contribution to team's advantage
Administrator	'What a nitpicker'	Wishes everybody were like this	'Bureaucrat'	Wants administrator to be nice to others about the rules
Entrepreneur	Crazy, lazy or rowing upstream	'This guy is off the wall'	Finds the other entrepreneur arrogant and stubborn	Always hoping that he/she is not creating uproar
Integrator	Doesn't add any value	Suspicious, feels undermined	Good guy	Suspicious of political power

The first step is to identify who typically plays what role(s). Things to take into consideration are work habits, behaviour and attitude towards others. Bear in mind that the four roles described are generic and that individuals tend to represent combinations of roles.

Next, the organization's stage in the corporate life cycle should be ascertained. The corporate life cycle does not necessarily describe the age of an organization, but rather its current vitality. In other words, a 100-year-old company could be in the adolescent stage, whereas a five-year-old company might have passed its prime already. Major organizational changes can also affect the 'age' of an organization.

Adizes identifies 10 stages of the corporate life cycle, analogous to that of humans:

1. courtship (ideas, making plans)

2. infancy (pursuing opportunity, taking risks)

3. go-go (rapid growth, sales focus)

4. adolescence (ownership versus leadership)

5. prime (balance between control and flexibility)

6. stability (control takes over)

7. aristocracy (resting on laurels)

8. recrimination (finger-pointing)

9. bureaucracy (the living dead company)

10. death (out of cash).

Each stage poses a unique combination of organizational characteristics, and so represents different opportunities for management roles to have a positive impact on organizational effectiveness.

Two key organizational dimensions follow from these life stages, namely long-term versus short-term orientation, and internal versus external orientation (see figure). By adjusting the weight of each role, the management team can be better 'geared' to deal with a certain situation. The third and final step is thus to compare and link the organization's current and desired management role mixes.

On a microscale, a business unit or organizational department can use the same steps to identify available roles, assess the current situation and ascertain the importance of certain roles at a given moment.

The final analysis

For decades, there has been an ongoing discussion about organisational life cycles and how they determine the need for certain management styles and roles. Though over 20 years old, Adizes' PAEI model is practical, simple and

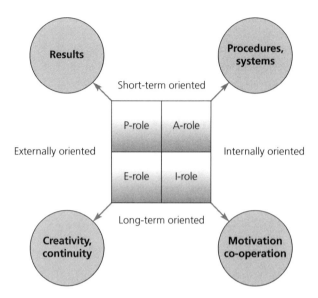

still one of the most commonly used. One of the key values of the PAEI model is in its ability to allow people to understand and appreciate the importance of different roles – and their conflicts – in an organization.

On a critical note, it is all too easy to force people into roles, either on paper or in perception: 'he is a typical P' or 'she is such an A'. Despite multiple warnings against one-role-for-one-person linkages, it is as easy to identify a person with a role as it is to read into your horoscope and interpret it to be true. Instead, roles can – and probably should – be played by more than one person.

Ansoff's product/market grid

The big idea

Ansoff's (1987) product/market expansion grid is a framework for identifying corporate growth opportunities. Two dimensions determine the scope of options (growth vectors), namely products and markets. Four generic growth strategies follow from Ansoff's matrix:

- **Market penetration**. Denotes a growth direction through the increase of market share for the current product-market combination.
- **Market development**. Refers to the pursuit of new missions (markets, channels) for current products.
- **Product development**. The development of new products to replace or complement current products.
- **Diversification**. Where both the product and the market are new to the corporation.

Within the diversification quadrant itself a variety of more specific growth vectors can be identified, based on how 'different' the new product and/or market are:

- **horizontal diversification** – when new (technologically unrelated) products are introduced to current markets;
- **vertical integration** – when an organization decides to move into its supplier's or customer's business to secure supply or firm up the use of its products in end products;
- **concentric diversification** – when new products closely related to current products are introduced into (new) markets;
- **conglomerate diversification** – when completely new, technologically unrelated products are introduced into new markets.

New	**2. Market development**	Concentric diversification	Conglomerate diversification
		4. Diversification	
		Vertical integration	
		Horizontal integration	
Markets	**1. Market penetration**	**3. Product development**	
Current			
	Current		New

Products

When to use it

The firm's product-market scope, its intended growth vector and its distinctive competitive advantage to succeed together describe its logical (strategic) path in the external environment. There is, however, more to Ansoff's grid.

As a fourth strategy component, Ansoff suggests considering a firm's ability to benefit from a new product-market entry through harnessing synergy. This can be done in two ways: by making use of an existing outstanding competence (aggressive synergy strategy), or by developing or acquiring the requisite competence (defensive synergy strategy).

Finally, there is the question of 'make or buy'. This refers to the corporate strategic option of embarking on integrative and diversified growth beyond the current scope of business by means of acquisition(s).

Ansoff's matrix thus covers five components of corporate business strategy:

1. product/market scope
2. growth vector
3. competitive advantage
4. synergy
5. make or buy.

Used in conjunction with an organization's business objectives, any number of these components can be used to outline its business strategy.

The final analysis

Despite being nearly half a century old, Ansoff's matrix is nonetheless still valid, and is frequently applied by marketing strategists. In fact, revisiting his work makes one realize that some of today's gurus have either reinvented the wheel or stolen it from him.

Used in isolation, the model can do little to help determine the best strategy, and the question as to which strategy would be most beneficial for a company is still generally left unanswered. Rather, the grid serves as a means to describe product-market opportunities and strategic options. As such, it forms an excellent framework for exploration, description and strategic dialogue.

The balanced scorecard

The big idea

The *balanced scorecard* essentially uses integral performance measurement to track and adjust business strategy. In addition to the usual financial perspective, it forces the manager to incorporate the customer perspective, operations and the organization's innovation and learning ability.

The balanced scorecard makes it possible to see aggregate financial consequences of non-financial measures that drive long-term financial success:

- What is important for our shareholders?
- How do customers perceive us?
- Which internal processes can add value?
- Are we innovative and ready for the future?

When to use it

The actual balanced scorecard measurements depend upon the nature of the company. For each perspective, we have made a non-exhaustive list of examples.

Financial perspective

Is the company's choice of strategy, its implementation and its execution contributing to the bottom line?

- operating income
- ROI, ROCE, EVA (or any other return rate)
- sales and revenue growth

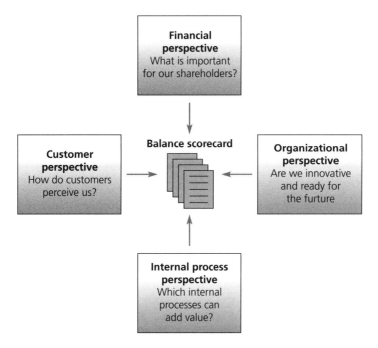

- repeat sales as a percentage of total sales volume
- product/customer/channel profitability
- revenue per unit/ton/customer/employee
- cost per unit (see Activity-based costing)
- sales costs as a percentage of total costs or revenues.

Customer perspective

How are our efforts as regards service and customer satisfaction affecting our top and bottom line?

- market share in target segment(s)
- existing customer business development
- customer profitability
- timely and damage-free delivery
- return policy
- claims and complaints handling
- handling service calls.

Internal process perspective

How successful is the company at setting up and managing business processes to meet (future) customer demands and deliver service?

- new sales as a percentage of total sales
- meeting product introduction goals
- product development cycle
- break-even time realized.

Learning and growth perspective

Are we successfully managing, developing and retaining human resources, knowledge and systems?

- employee satisfaction and retention, or the opposite (turnover rate)
- revenue and/or value added per employee
- strategic redundancy in job skills (job-coverage ratio)
- employee retraining cycle time
- new ideas (per employee, implemented)
- information availability relative to need.

The final analysis

There is nothing new about the call for measurement of non-financial measures, but Kaplan and Norton (1993) can be given credit for being advocates of a more balanced impact of these measures. A CEO is relatively more likely to be biased towards financial measures than, let's say, a marketing assistant. Lower in an organization, people are more likely to use non-financial measures.

The BCG matrix

The big idea

To ensure long-term success, a company should have a portfolio of products that contains both high-growth products in need of cash inputs and low-growth products that generate excess cash. Or at least, that is the assumption made by the Boston Consulting Group (BCG) underlying its popular matrix.

The BCG matrix helps to determine priorities in a product portfolio. Its basic premise is that it makes more sense to invest where there is (economic) growth from which you can benefit. A rating of products on two dimensions, market share and market growth, creates four qualifications of products in your portfolio: stars, cash cows, question marks (or wild cats) and dogs.

When to use it

For each product or service in your portfolio (or scope of analysis), determine (a measure or rating of) expected relative market growth.

Next, what is your relative market share for each product? Apply a percentage or a rating.

Plot all products on the two dimensions and apply a division on both dimensions, based on a arbitrary, but consistent difference between relatively big and relatively small. This is the hardest part. Predetermined criteria can help. For example: our market share is small when our share is less than one-third of that of the biggest competitor. Or for the other dimension: the market's growth rate is high when annual revenues grow by more than 10 per cent after correction for inflation. It is important to not change these criteria around in order to shift 'pet' projects and products into more favorable grounds, thereby defeating the purpose of the exercise.

Stars are products that enjoy a relatively high market share in a strongly growing market. They are (potentially) profitable and may grow further to become an important product or category for the company. You should focus on and invest in these products.

Although the market is no longer growing, your **cash cows** have a relatively high market share and bring in healthy profits. No efforts or investments are necessary to maintain the status quo.

Although their market share is relatively small, the market for **question marks** is growing rapidly. Investments to create growth may yield big results in the future, though this is far from certain. Further investigation into how and where to invest is advised.

Drop or divest the **dogs** when they are not profitable. If profitable, do not invest, but make the best out of its current value. This may even mean selling the product's operations and/or brand.

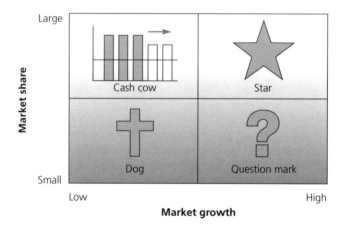

The final analysis

Many people have questioned the relative ease with which the BCG matrix assumes that markets are clearly defined, that market shares are good indicators of cash generation and that growth means that cash infusions are needed to extract a bigger payoff at a later stage. Most importantly, say many critics, throwing money at a product or product group by itself does not make it grow or become profitable. Our conclusion is that the BCG matrix can be very helpful in forcing decisions in managing a portfolio of products. However, it cannot be employed as the sole means of determining strategies for a portfolio of products.

When constructing a matrix, it often makes more sense to use relative market shares or even ratings, as markets are not always clearly defined.

They can be heterogeneous, with many substitute products. Markets can be concentrated or widely divided among many small players. Also, keep in mind that, especially in immature markets, growth figures and markets shares may not have reached a balance that justifies the rigorously positive or negative judgment of the BCG matrix.

Belbin's team roles

The big idea

Belbin (1985) derived the concept of nine distinct and interdependent team roles from his study of successful and unsuccessful teams competing in business games.

According to Belbin, a team role is 'a tendency to behave, contribute and interrelate with others in a particular way'. In order to be successful, a team and its members need to fulfil the following complementary nine roles:

- shaper
- implementer
- completer/finisher
- co-ordinator
- team worker
- resource investigator
- 'plant'/creator/inventor
- monitor/evaluator
- specialist.

Belbin states that team members with complementary roles are 'richer' and more successful.

When to use it

In order to make use of the model, members of a prospective team should first determine which roles they can and want to fulfil.

Each member should subsequently be assessed using the following indicators to see whether, and to what extent they can play one or more of the following nine roles:

The **co-ordinator** is a mature and confident person. He or she probably brings to the table experience as a chairman or leader of some kind. This person clarifies goals, encourages decision-making, and delegates tasks, but can, however, be manipulative or bossy, especially when he or she lets others do work that could and should be done by himself/herself.

The **team worker** is co-operative, mild, perceptive and diplomatic. In a nutshell: everybody's friend. The team worker listens, builds, balances, and averts friction. His or her inherent indecisiveness surfaces in crunch situations. The doers in the team tend to think the team worker talks too much.

Cerebral roles

The team roles of four people (in this illustration represented by different types of lines) together cover most of the nine roles required for successful team work.

The **resource investigator** is an enthusiastic, communicative extrovert who explores opportunities and develops contacts that he thinks will benefit him/her now or later. Although opportunistic and optimistic, the resource investigator tends to have a short span of attention and quickly loses interest.

The **'plant'** is Belbin's name for the creator or inventor. The plant is creative and imaginative, brilliant at times. His or her unorthodox thinking helps to solve difficult problems. The plant ignores incidentals and is too preoccupied to communicate effectively. The problem is that this self-aware genius has a tendency to get other team members' backs up.

The **monitor** evaluates actions and ponders the strategy. The person is sober, yet discerning and keeps track of progress. He or she oversees all options and judges accurately, but lacks drive and ability to inspire others.

The **specialist** is a single-minded, dedicated self-starter. The specialist provides rare knowledge and skills so his/her contribution is limited to a narrow front. This person gets a kick out of technicalities and needs to be told to get to the point.

The **shaper** is challenging, dynamic, and thrives on pressure. He or she has the drive and courage to overcome obstacles, sees no evil, hears no evil. The shaper might rub people the wrong way in his/her zealous efforts get things going. Don't people share the shaper's vision?

The **implementer** is disciplined, reliable, conservative and efficient, and turns ideas into practical actions. Once at work, the implementer will keep going and stick to the plan. This person might be a little rigid and unwilling to adapt alternative approaches or solutions along the way.

The **finisher** is meticulous, punctual, conscientious and anxious to make sure everything turns out perfect. The finisher delivers on time, but sometimes worries too much. He or she certainly hates to delegate work. Nobody else seems to understand that it has to be perfect.

The assessment can be done in various ways:

- self-assessment (apply scores, rank, rate or distribute weights), possibly overseen by a third party;
- team assessment (let the team work on a small assignment or game and let the members grade each other);
- assessment by mentor, co-worker or supervisor, former team members, etc.

With a profile of each team member's ability to fulfil one or more roles, potential under or overrepresentation of certain roles in the team can be detected. If necessary, management may decide to use this information to reshuffle the team.

Analysis of team members using the Belbin model is especially useful in situations where a team must be created to undertake an assignment that requires a certain set of skills and combination of roles.

Such an assessment is in itself beneficial in that it encourages individuals to take a closer look at themselves, and at their strengths and weaknesses. These can then be exploited or corrected as appropriate, ultimately resulting in a more flexible and thus stronger team.

The final analysis

Belbin's way of looking at teams and the roles of team members assumes that there is an objective basis upon which one can assess team members. Although arbitrary, it is nonetheless a very useful exercise.

People will recognize themselves and team dynamics in this model. Just as different roles are complementary, it can be fatal to have too many representatives of the same type of role in one team: too many co-ordinators clash, two monitors keep waiting for the other to do something and two team workers talk too much.

What the model does not address is the importance of interpersonal relationships within a team. A lot of teams that look good on paper fail to function properly in practice because there is no 'click'. The reverse is also true: for example, a person who has no history of being a co-ordinator may rise to the occasion and fill up a vacuum. To a large degree, the roles are thus relative to each other.

Benchmarking

The big idea

Benchmarking is the systematic comparison of organizational processes and performances in order to create new standards and/or improve processes. There are four basic types:

- internal – benchmarking within an organization, e.g. between business units;
- competitive – benchmarking operations and performance with direct competitors;
- functional – benchmarking similar processes within the broader range of the industry;
- generic – comparing operations between unrelated industries.

All types of benchmarking can be very rewarding: they can provide new insights into strengths and weaknesses of (parts of) an organization, illustrate possible improvements, objective norms, new guidelines and fresh ideas.

When to use it

Much has been written on the methodology of the benchmarking process. Most variations on the basic elements of the methodology are the result of including situational characteristics or explanatory factors to account for differences, forward-looking industry analyses or simply practical issues that arise in certain industries or in communication between benchmarking partners and analysts.

Benchmarking entails the following (sometimes overlapping) steps:

- Determine the scope.
- Choose the benchmark partner(s).

- Determine measure(s), units, indicators and data collection method.
- Collect data.
- Analyse the discrepancies – get facts behind the numbers.
- Present the analysis and discuss implications in terms of (new) goals.
- Make an action plan and/or procedures.
- Monitor progress in ongoing benchmark.

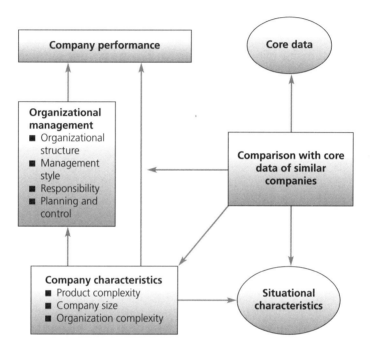

The first question is: what do we want to achieve with the benchmarking project? Bearing in mind the difference between intention and action, we can define the purpose as an answer to either one or more of the following questions:

- How good are we at what we do?
- Are we as good as others at what we do?
- How can we do what we do better?
- Of course, one should be aware of the difference between intention and action in this respect.

When determining the scope of the benchmarking exercise, consider the client impact and communicability of the project in order to increase the rate of success, as well as the effort required to realize a valuable benchmark.

Ideally, the benchmarking partner is considered to be performing at least equally as well or better. Potential partners are often identified through industry experts and publications.

Quite often, differences in products, processes and management make comparison difficult, if not impossible. Berenschot uses the BETTI® Benchmark model, depicted in the figure. This particular variation of benchmarking accounts for explanatory factors or situational characteristics that define the company's situation, e.g. a complex product or very wide assortment. Performance indicators can be adjusted using the situational characteristics, to allow for a 'fair' comparison and derive the improvement potential for each particular performance indicator.

An example of such an explanatory factor is product complexity. If your company has a higher product complexity, e.g. in terms of number of parts or actions, than that of the benchmark partner, that could (partially) explain a lower on-time completion reliability. Not only can an analyst use multiple benchmarks to derive an approximation of the 'benchmark' for your company, the very determination of the explanatory factor triggers an improvement opportunity. In this example, a lower number of parts or actions could increase on-time completion reliability.

Site visits to the benchmark partner, as well as mutual interest in the benchmarking project increase the rate of success of benchmarking significantly. Warning: the buzzword to describe unprepared or non-specific benchmarking visits is 'industrial tourism'.

The final analysis

Benchmarking is not easy. All too often, benchmarking is carried out by semi-committed managers, without the use of predetermined measures, and without the proper tools for analysis and presentation. Unquestionably, many benchmarking projects end in dismay, a futile exercise often justifiably portrayed by onlookers as industrial tourism, comparing apples and pears. Even when performed in a structured way, the 'they're different from us' syndrome prevents benchmarking from leading to changes for the better. Furthermore, competitive sensitivity can stifle the free flow of information, even within an organization.

By applying explanatory factors, benchmarking can not only provide comparative data that can trigger the need for improvement, but also highlight new improvement opportunities and solutions to problems. For this very reason, Berenschot argues that the differences between benchmark partners should be embraced, rather than trying to exclude 'non-comparable' products or processes.

Benchmarking is never ending: apart from having to measure continuously in order to get up to date results, the competition is not going to stand still! The argument that benchmarking at best can only ever result in catch-up performance can be countered with three facts: companies generally benchmark the best performer, benchmarking sparks many new ideas, and – perhaps most importantly – customers may not (yet) be willing to pay for a product or service that is better than that currently provided by the best performer.

A producer and distributor of office products for professional customers based in the North of England had grown internationally as a result of acquisitions. Facing stronger competition on an international level, our client wanted to perform an internal benchmark study. The different operations throughout Europe were to be compared in order to identify best practices and subsequent improvements (phase 1) and synergy opportunities (phase 2).

The entire company's cost structure and human resources were within the scope of the benchmark study. For each functional process, a set of output/input (O/I) indicators was defined. Explanatory factors enabled fair interpretation and comparison of comparison data. Using the explanatory factors, the 12 operating companies were divided into three groups within which companies could be compared. As the methodology and I/O indicators were the same for each group, a full comparison of 12 companies was possible at a later stage.

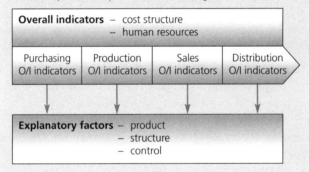

For each of the 12 operating companies, the benchmarking process included:

- an introductory workshop, outlining current developments and plans for improvement;
- drawing up a questionnaire to collect all relevant data;
- management interviews (two days);
- review of business plans, plus additional interviews;
- benchmark analysis, comparing data;
- identification of 'best practices';
- determination of improvement potential per process per company;
- final workshop with presentation of planned improvements and expected results.

The Berenschot project management model

The big idea

The *Berenschot project management model* identifies a number of aspects to be borne in mind when carrying out any project, thereby greatly simplifying what can only be described as an inherently complex process. The four areas for consideration are as follows:

- **The life cycle** – this refers to all the stages within the 'life' of a project, from definition through to execution and 'after-care'.
- **The project hierarchy** – all but the simplest projects consist of a number of sub-projects. Understanding the interrelationships between the various sub-projects can be invaluable in determining interdependencies and thus priorities.
- **The project fundamentals** – answering the following questions before embarking on a project can be of great help in ensuring that it achieves its purpose both on time and within budget:
  - What is the ultimate objective of the project and what do you hope to achieve through its realization?
  - What means (tools, people and methods) do you have at your disposal, and what practical issues need to be addressed in this regard?
  - What are the project specifications and how can success/failure be measured?
  - How can you ensure that you deliver quality?
  - What is the timeline?
  - What is your budget?
  - How do you intend to organize the project?
  - How do you intend to inform participants about the project?

- How are you going to handle publicity generally?
- The degree of detail in the answers to each of these questions will of course vary from phase to phase as the project progresses. What is important is that the answers remain consistent.

■ **The management cycle** – four repetitive steps for continuous improvement and learning: Plan, Do, Check and Act (see The Deming cycle later in this book). Having planned and carried out the various activities, the results should be examined and checked against the master plan on an ongoing basis. Any improvements/ alterations can be implemented as necessary.

The first three dimensions are necessary in order to define, start up and carry out a project, while the last of the four, the management cycle, is important to ensure controlled execution of the whole.

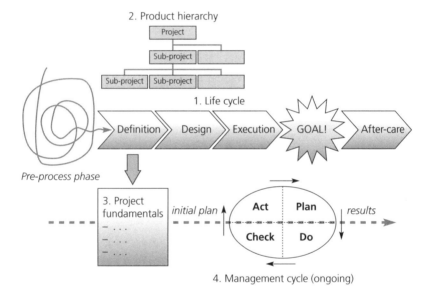

When to use it

Regardless of the degree of complexity of the project in question, the concept of the Berenschot project management model is easy to grasp. It is, furthermore, relatively easy to apply: simply go through the bulleted list above and ensure that sufficient attention has been devoted to each.

Finally, it is important not to forget the stakeholders – consider who stands to gain from success or failure of the project and how they might (try to) affect the outcome.

The final analysis

The danger of a model such as this is that it can offer a false sense of secu-
rity: after all, having gone through all the motions with such care, how
can a project possibly fail? At the end of the day, though, correct use of the
model is not a *guarantee* for success, but a *condition*.

Business process redesign

The big idea

Business process redesign (BPR) gurus Hammer and Champy (1993) define BPR as the fundamental reconsideration and radical redesign of organizational processes, in order to achieve drastic improvement of current performance in cost, quality, service and speed. Value creation for the customer is the leading factor for process redesign, in which information technology often plays an important role.

There are generally five important rules to keep in mind with any BPR project:

1. Determine strategy before redesigning.
2. Use the primary process as a basis.
3. Optimize the use of information technology.
4. Organizational structure and governance models must be compatible with the primary process.

In addition, there is a general condition for success, namely that management and employees must participate.

Often, the redesign entails a 'back to square one' approach. In an effort to allow discussion of any new views on how to design the organization, the existing organizational structure and processes are considered 'nonexistent', or irrelevant in the redesign.

When to use it

Before engaging in a BPR project, the organization must come to the realization that there is a need for BPR. Consequently, the very first step is determining the scope of the BPR project, or even more fundamentally,

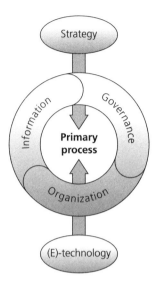

deciding if there is a need for BPR at all. The BPR team should determine this need by assessing indicators such as:

- numerous conflicts within (parts of) the organization;
- unusually high frequency of meetings;
- excessive amount of non-structured communication (memos, e-mails, announcements, etc.).

Successful BPR projects executed by Berenschot consultants have yielded such remarkable results as:
- 70% reduction in order delivery time
- 60% reduction in average inventory level
- 25% increase in revenues
- 50% reduction in indirect labour
- 98% delivery reliability, up from 70%.

One way to determine whether or not there are too many conflicts or whether or not meetings and additional communication are excessive is by benchmarking the organization or department with another.

Having established the need, the next step in the BPR process is the redesigning of (part of) the organization in accordance with strategic requirements. Ask:

- What is the focus of our efforts (think about products, services and target customers)?

- What are the critical success factors?
- How can we achieve maximum efficiency based on the required output levels?

The third step is determining the required management of the newly designed organization. Typical questions here are:

- How can we ensure that processes will function as intended?
- How can we measure performance?
- How can we adjust for improvements, if needed?
- How can we compensate or reward?

The last step comprises the implementation of the new organizational structure, the installation of management and procedures, and the integration of the organization's work methods into its environment.

The final analysis

BPR is much more difficult to do than to describe. Lack of sufficient project management, limited management support and 'delegating' BPR projects to the IT department are fatal, yet prevalent causes of BPR project failure. Another problem with BPR is that, though it makes sense on the 'hard' side, getting people to work within a new structure, under new rules, proves to be more challenging than anticipated. Many BPR projects stall in the design phase.

Neither redesigning organizational structures and processes, nor implementing new technologies as part of a BPR project will automatically remedy all flaws in an organization, let alone offer a permanent, sustainable solution. That is the very reason why employees, management and an organization's culture are called the 'key enablers' of BPR.

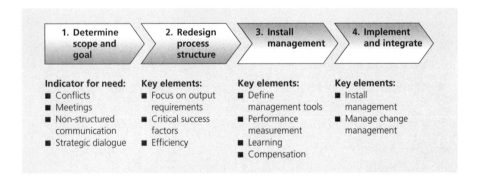

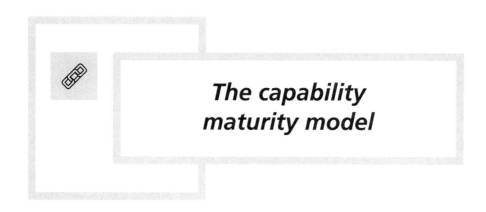

The capability maturity model

The big idea

Have you ever wondered why that expensive new system did not pay off as much as expected? The *capability maturity model* provides insight into the stage of development of maturity of an organization for software development.

This model describes five evolutionary levels of ways in which the organization manages its processes. Specific steps and activities to get from one level to the next are provided. The most ominous message is that the organization should be able to 'carry' its software applications.

When to use it

Use the capability maturity model to determine which of the following describes your organization best:

1. **Initial.** The development process is characterized as *ad hoc*, occasionally chaotic. Few processes are defined, and success depends on individual efforts.

2. **Repeatable.** Basic project management processes are established to track cost, schedule, and functionality. The necessary process discipline is in place to repeat earlier successes on projects with similar applications.

3. **Defined.** The software process for both management and engineering activities is documented, standardized, and integrated into a standard software process for the organization. All projects use an approved, tailored version of the organization's standard software process for developing and maintaining software.

4. **Managed.** Detailed measures of the software process and product quality are collected. Both the software process and products are quantitatively understood and controlled.

5. **Optimizing.** Continuous process improvement is enabled by quantitative feedback from the process and from piloting innovative ideas and technologies.

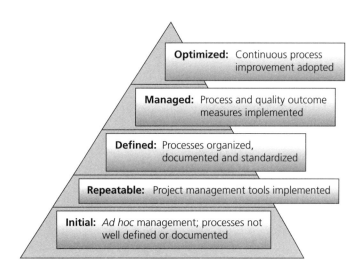

Predictability, effectiveness, and control of an organization's software processes are believed to improve as the organization moves up the five levels.

Except for Level 1, each maturity level is further split up into several key process areas that indicate the areas on which an organization should focus to improve its software process.

The key process areas at Level 2 focus on the software project's concerns related to establishing basic project management controls. They are Requirements Management, Software Project Planning, Software Project Tracking and Oversight, Software Subcontract Management, Software Quality Assurance, and Software Configuration Management.

The key process areas at Level 3 address both project and organizational issues, as the organization establishes an infrastructure that institutionalizes effective software engineering and management processes across all projects. They are Organization Process Focus, Organization Process Definition, Training Programmes, Integrated Software Management, Software Product Engineering, Intergroup Coordination, and Peer Reviews.

The key process areas at Level 4 focus on establishing a quantitative understanding of both the software process and the software work products being built. They are Quantitative Process Management and Software Quality Management.

The key process areas at Level 5 cover the issues that both the organization and the projects must address to implement continual, measurable software process improvement. They are Defect Prevention, Technology Change Management, and Process Change Management.

Each key process area is described in terms of the key practices that contribute to satisfying its goals. The key practices describe the infrastructure and activities that contribute most to the effective implementation and institutionalization of the key process area.

The final analysis

The capability maturity model is a very accessible model that can be used not only for analysis and evaluation of the organization and its software applications, but also as a basis for organizational improvements. Thanks to the relevance of its pragmatic five levels to both process improvement issues and organizational development in general, the capability maturity model thus rises above its original IT nature.

The model does require a high level of understanding of various organizational elements and how they are related, such as IT, strategy and process management, in addition to which it focuses on the 'hard' side of managing an organization. Effective organizational improvements require additional models and insights that shed some light on the human aspect or the 'soft' side.

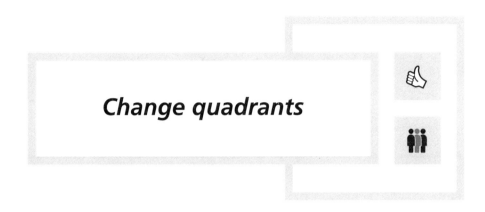

Change quadrants

The big idea

The *change quadrants model* helps management to define an approach for successfully managing organizational change. The change quadrants can be useful in determining the change agents, identifying active participants in the change process, and establishing the scope of change and the timing in order to maximize the success of change efforts.

The basic premise is that the approach for change depends on whether an organization is 'warm' or 'cold', and whether the change is 'warm' or 'cold':

- A **cold** organization is one where rules, regulations, systems, structures and procedures drive direction, control and co-ordination to get results; there is little or no intrinsic willingness to (out)perform. In a **warm** organization, however, it is shared norms and values, and a common understanding of direction that make the organization work.

- A **cold** change is the result of an objectively discernible situation or emergency, such as a near bankruptcy, a drastic drop in market share, revenues, profits or an unavoidable (new) competitive threat. A **warm** change, on the other hand, is primarily driven by personal and professional ambitions.

Based on the various warm/cold combinations of organization and change, there are four possible change strategies: intervention, implementation, transformation and innovation.

When to use it

The model of change quadrants is qualitatively constructed for each company, drawn up on the basis of interviews with key figures within the organization. Besides the warm/cold typology, our experience with change processes has revealed several underlying dimensions that also need to be investigated: necessity of change, momentum, resistance to change, culture and empowerment.

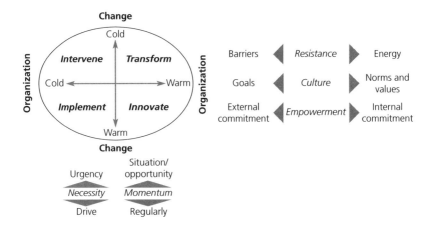

Change: cold or warm?

The *necessity of change* can be fuelled by either urgency (external) or drive (from within). *Momentum*, on the other hand, can be generated as a result of a particular situation or opportunity, for example, during a merger or a recession. There could also be a regularly reoccurring momentum, for example, in seasonal industries.

Organization: cold or warm?

Organizational resistance is generally passive, in which case it is relatively easy to overcome through education, training and new resources. However, energy from within the organization actively directed against change is harder to beat and thus requires a much tougher change management approach.

Some *organizational cultures* have an explicit focus on objectives, results or targets. Others, however, may rely on norms and values for guidance.

The *empowerment* dimension makes a distinction between external and internal commitment: in the former, people simply do as they're told, whereas in the latter, individuals act and decide with the best interests of the company in mind.

A common mistake is to try to force a warm change through a cold organization. People may not be as committed to the company and as willing to change as management thinks, as a result of which nothing really happens. The problem is that the next time management wants to change something, there may be even less support.

Imposing a cold change on a warm organization can be even more damaging: the erosion of hitherto strong commitment can result in a strong negative response that may cause irreparable damage to the company.

The final analysis

The change quadrants model is used often in conjunction with other models and change management approaches, for example Kotter's (1990) Eight Phases of Change.

In addition to the change quadrants, management's preferences and style should also be reflected in the change management approach. Not only a mismatch between organization and proposed change, but also emotion and the personal style of management may obstruct the process. Bear in mind that a 'cold' change is easier to plan and communicate than a 'warm' one, and also that many organizations deem themselves 'warmer' than they really are.

On the flip-side of the 'prescription' for warm or cold change, organizations should not exclude the option of 'warming up' or 'cooling down' before going through a change process, be it warm or cold.

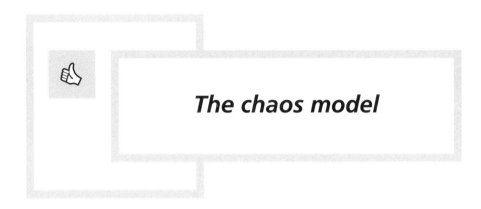

The chaos model

The big idea

Chaos is an essential stage in any fundamental change process that leads to self-organization. In fact, argues Zuijderhoudt (1990, 1992, 2000), trying to prevent chaos is damaging to an organization's ability to move up to a higher level of independence and dynamic self-organization. The process of dynamic self-organization is illustrated in the chaos model.

Under normal circumstances, an organization finds itself in a relatively stable situation of 'manageable' development. Then comes a more dynamic period, in which agents of innovation and change cause fluctuations in the organization's ability to cope with internal and external developments: certain (groups of) people in the organization fail to catch up in the change process and/or disagree with the changes, the rationale behind the changes, or the messenger of the changes. The crucial point of entry into chaos is when the decision is made to *not* try to control the process anymore, but instead to allow the organization to try to find its own solution.

Assuming that the organization manages to emerge from the chaos, there are three possibilities:

- The organization returns to its old order as the need for change declines and preferential fluctuations dwindle.
- A new 'germ' or 'core' buds and is supported by a large enough coalition, creating a new 'synergy'.
- Regression: the organization fails to find a solution and returns to its old ways and/or disintegrates.

Many organizations are able to remain temporarily in a state of ongoing preferential fluctuations and chaos, consuming large amounts of organizational energy.

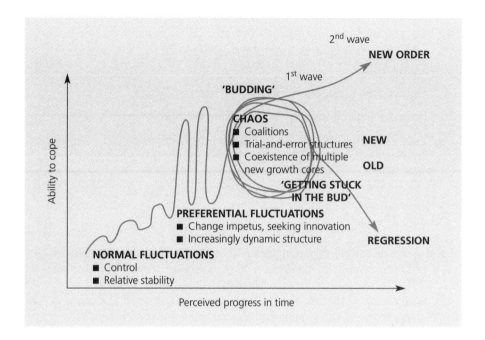

The chaos model diagram showing "Ability to cope" (vertical axis) against "Perceived progress in time" (horizontal axis).

- 2nd wave → **NEW ORDER**
- 1st wave
- **'BUDDING'**
- **CHAOS**
  - Coalitions
  - Trial-and-error structures — **NEW**
  - Coexistence of multiple new growth cores — **OLD**
- **'GETTING STUCK IN THE BUD'**
- **PREFERENTIAL FLUCTUATIONS**
  - Change impetus, seeking innovation
  - Increasingly dynamic structure — **REGRESSION**
- **NORMAL FLUCTUATIONS**
  - Control
  - Relative stability

When to use it

When used as more than a metaphor for complex and paradoxical organi-zational change processes, and taken beyond self-reflection, this model may help leaders to let go of their desire to fully 'control' change, and leave room for self-organization.

The application of chaos theory in organizational analysis and inter-vention can be found in the attitude changes of leaders:

- letting go of the desire to control;
- giving way to self-organization;
- not trying to make explicit use of theory in the face of anticipated obstruction of abstract concepts ('nasty questions').

Many leaders, managers and consultants think of an organization as a collection of consciously chosen and well-maintained (transactional) rela-tionships of goods, funds and information. Using chaos theory explicitly requires letting go of the preconceived notion of ability to apply and con-trol changes over such relationships.

To explain how to use chaos theory would imply that there is a need to manage, or even control, the process of change. However, it is important to understand when to let the organization go, and when to intervene. The leader and/or consultant should be able to recognize the generic phases to 'time' the intervention: control, chaos and 'stuck.'

Four steps are suggested for the use of the chaos theory in organiza-tional change:

1. Investigate (diagnose) the nature of change dynamics in the organization.

2. Make problems explicit (but don't imply solutions!).

3. Formulate a change impetus: let chaos happen.

4. Offer limited guidance (more support, less management, very little control) in realizing the breakthrough solution: allow for self-organization.

The final analysis

The chaos and complexity theory suffers from incomplete use. More often than not, the model is used as a metaphor or frame of reference to (vaguely) describe certain processes of organizational change.

In many cases, the theory is used, but not named, because of its abstract nature and the absence of 'logical' cause-and-effect links.

Competing values of organizational effectiveness

The big idea

Do organizational researchers share an implicit theoretical framework as regards organizational effectiveness? In a two-stage study, Quinn and Rohrbaugh (1983) empanelled organizational theorists and researchers to make judgments about the similarity of commonly used effectiveness criteria. The authors started with a carefully chosen list of indices of organizational effectiveness. Using the panel members' paired comparison ratings, they produced a pool of fundamental cognitive dimensions with the individual judgments of relative similarity or dissimilarity.

The result of the study was a multidimensional scaling or spatial model with three dimensions:

- internal versus external organizational focus
- flexibility versus stability of the organization
- process (means) versus goals (ends) orientation.

These three dimensions reflect some key topics of debate in the management and research of organizations.

The first dimension, internal versus external organizational focus, represents a basic organizational dilemma, in which at one end of the scale the organization is viewed as a socio-technical entity, and at the other as a logically designed tool to accomplish business goals.

Flexibility versus stability is another basic organizational dilemma. Order and control do not mix well with innovation and change. Many social theorists have (successfully) argued for authority, structure, and co-ordination, while others have found wide support for individual initiative and organizational adaptability.

Finally, on the third dimension, a study of organizational effectiveness cannot be complete without observation of the tendency of means,

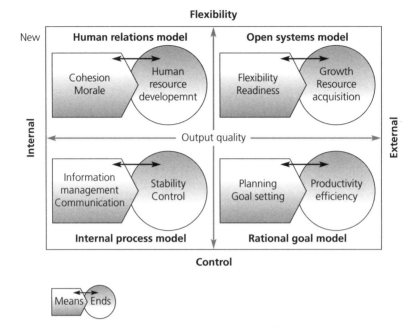

methods, procedures and rules to become functionally autonomous, i.e. become goals in themselves.

The three-dimensional integration of these three continual results in four basic models of organizational effectiveness:

- human relations model
- open systems model
- internal process model
- rational goal model.

Quinn and Rohrbaugh present a number of alternative methods to compare and describe their model, for instance, Parson's functional prerequisites model, in which core values, co-ordination mechanisms and organizational structures are presented.

When to use it

This model helps organizational theorists to better structure and understand the key dilemmas facing organizations in pursuit of maximized effectiveness.

The final analysis

Debate on model to describe organizations and the issues they face is ongoing. In an effort to derive a framework for organizational analysis, Quinn and Rohrbaugh approached a large number of organizational researchers and experts to determine the key dimensions of organizational issues. The fact that the three dimensions of the model so closely describe three major areas of debate and research indicates that the authors have been quite successful in their effort to provide a framework for organizational effectiveness.

In anticipation of criticism, Quinn and Rohrbaugh agree that the spatial model is a type of oxymoron, a combination of seemingly contradictory or ingenuous concepts. But the theoretical paradoxes are not necessarily empirical opposites. They argue that an organization might be cohesive and productive, or stable as well as flexible. In line with another often-heard complaint with regard to models such as this, it is noted that the elimination of criteria to construct dimensions for a framework for organizational effectiveness represents a key discussion surrounding the whole concept of (management) models: does simplification limit the researcher's perspective? Quinn and Rohrbaugh would seem to argue the contrary, as they state that the process of creating the model is, in fact, generative.

Competitive analysis: Porter's five forces

The big idea

Porter's (1998) competitive analysis identifies five fundamental competitive forces that determine the relative attractiveness of an industry: new entrants, bargaining power of buyers, bargaining power of suppliers, substitute products or services, and rivalry among existing competitors. Competitive analysis leads to insight in relationships and dynamics in an industry, and allows a company or business unit to make strategic decisions regarding the best defendable and most economically attractive position.

When to use it

For each of the five forces, consider how well your company can compete.

1. New entrants

Are there entry barriers for new contenders?

- The higher the importance of economies of scale, the higher the entry barrier.
- Competing with established brands and loyalty is harder (e.g. Coca-Cola).
- High up-front (risky) capital requirements make entry difficult.
- High switching cost for products are of great advantage to existing players.
- Is access to distribution channels difficult or legally restricted?
- Do existing companies have scale-independent cost advantages (e.g. patents, licences, proprietary know-how, favourable access to raw materials, capital assets, experienced workers, subsidies)?

- A government-regulated industry could limit entry by requiring operating licences (e.g. UMTS wireless communication).
- Low expected retaliation by existing players makes entry easier for newcomers.
- The concept of 'entry deterring price': the bigger the margin, the more new entrants.

2. Substitutes

How easily can your product or service be substituted with another type of product or service? For example, the bus is a substitute for the train. Porter argues that a substitute is particularly threatening if it represents a significant improvement in the price/performance trade-off.

3. Buyer's bargaining power

To what extent can buyers bargain?

- When buyers buy in large volumes, they are more likely to command better prices. For example, large grocery retailers pay lower wholesale prices than small stores.
- The larger the fraction of costs represented by purchasing price, the harder buyers will bargain.
- Undifferentiated products make it easier to play suppliers against each other.
- Low switching costs increase buyer power.
- Low profit buyers will be tough negotiators.
- Potential 'do-it-ourselves' or backwards integration are strong bargaining levers. Partial in-house producing or 'tapered integration' not only is a strong bargaining instrument, it also gives better understanding of a supplier's actual costs!
- The less the buyer's performance is affected by the product, the more price sensitive the buyer.
- The more information a buyer has, the better his bargaining.

4. Supplier's command of industry

Suppliers can have a significant impact on the industry's profitability and margin distribution, depending on several levers. Competitive forces from suppliers mirror those of buyers:

- A few suppliers selling to relatively more buyers will be able to have a bigger say.
- The absence of substitutes increases supplier power as buyers have little choice.

- Suppliers with alternative customers, industries and channels have more power.
- The supplier's product is indispensable or of great value to your company.
- Switching suppliers will incur high expenses or rapidly depreciate your company's assets.
- Suppliers may integrate forwards by producing for and selling to your customers.

5. Existing competitors

Last, but not least, rivalry among existing competitors leads to tactics such as aggressive pricing and promotion, battles for customers or channels, increased service levels, etc. If moves and countermoves escalate (e.g. price wars), all industry rivals may end up losing. However, advertising battles may enhance differentiation in the industry for the benefit of all. Although rivalry and its intensity change as the industry furthers its marketing and technologies, the following are indicators of competitive threat from existing industry rivals:

- many and/or equally balanced competitors;
- slow industry growth, leading to focus over dividing, as opposed to growing the industry;
- high fixed cost and asset bases making rivals compete to turn stock and fill capacity;
- products perceived as commodity and imposing low switching cost on the buyer, a combination that causes shopping for price;
- large capacity increments only, causing major ups and downs in capacity discrepancies and, consequently, price (e.g. in chemical industries and semi-conductors);
- diversity of competitors and their strategies, making it difficult to anticipate competitive moves;
- high stakes, for example, to get a customer base in cellular communication or sales on the Internet;
- high exit barriers, for economic, strategic, emotional, or legal reasons. Major exit barriers are specialized assets that are difficult to sell, fixed cost of exit (e.g. labour agreements, settlement costs), and strategic importance of activities or brands for the corporation or its partners.

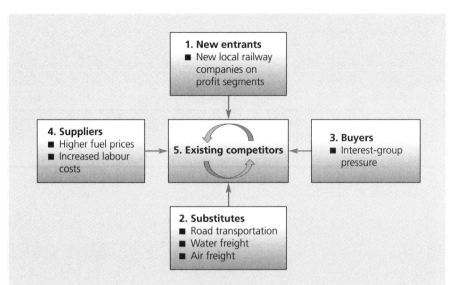

1. New entrants
- New local railway companies on profit segments

4. Suppliers
- Higher fuel prices
- Increased labour costs

5. Existing competitors

3. Buyers
- Interest-group pressure

2. Substitutes
- Road transportation
- Water freight
- Air freight

One of our clients, a national railway company, encountered many present and potential competitive forces that could be described using Porter's five forces model.

The market was being derogated and government subsidies to the monopolist declined rapidly. New local railway companies making timely entries into the market, focussing on the most profitable travel segments. Commercial customers could easily switch to road or water transportation to increase flexibility or lower costs, whichever was desired. At the same time, the company was facing pressure to increase its return on investment for a future public offering, but was also required by the government to maintain certain services. Advanced management of alternative transportation by means of regulated and private road transportation was starting to pose a serious threat to our client. Deregulation also invited foreign railway companies to explore the profitable opportunities in the client's domestic market. The company's personal travel customers were (and still are) represented by a powerful interest group. On the supplier side, fuel prices and labour costs were growing.

The model helped our client to identify and structure its competitive playing field as part of its strategy development process.

Note: the illustration and description have been altered so as to provide a suitable example and do not therefore represent all the relevant facts.

The final analysis

Although it is arguably the most widely used and recognized model for strategic analysis, this powerful model has one major disadvantage, namely that it tends to emphasize external forces and how they can be countered by the company in question. The organization's intrinsic strengths and ability to develop its competencies independently of these forces is a largely untouched aspect. The model can therefore be classified as reactive rather than pro-active, and is best used in combination with an inside-out approach.

Compliance typology

The big idea

Compliance is a key element of the relationship between those who have power and those over whom power is exercised.

Power secures compliance of others, whereas involvement determines the attitude of the subject toward the exercise of power. Depending on purpose, culture and member types, different types of power and different types of involvement can result in different types of compliance.

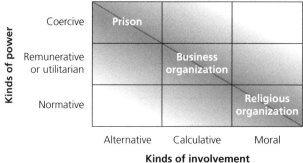

Kinds of involvement

Compliance patterns play an important role in organizational structure. Etzioni (1965) developed a typology for organizations based on compliance relations by combining three kinds of power with three kinds of involvement:

- **Coercive power** involves the potential use of physical force to make someone comply, such as in a master–slave relationship.

- **Remunerative** or **utilitarian power** is based on rewards and sanctions, for example, trade embargoes on countries that violate human rights.
- **Normative power** depends on a belief that authorities have a right to govern behaviour.
- **Alienative involvement** means that the power subject disagrees with the power holder and submits against his will in fear of physical pain or confinement.
- **Calculative involvement** refers to the subject's deliberate choice to comply in expectation of a reward or in avoidance of sanctions.
- **Moral involvement** is the result of agreement based on norms and values.

When plotted in a matrix, nine types of compliance emerge. The so-called congruent relations (1, 5 and 9) are found more frequently than the other six types because congruence is more effective and social units are under external and internal pressure to be effective. For example, coercive power may be the only effective power means in an organization where 'members' are highly alienated, but in an environment where members are committed, it is quite sure to have adverse effects.

Incongruent compliance relations do occur, however. Organizations have only limited control over the power applied and the involvement of participants. The successful exercise of power requires resources and skills, whereas involvement may depend on external factors that are beyond the control of the organization, such as religious norms and values, union memberships and personality structure.

Etzioni posted a few critical hypotheses on this theoretical groundwork:

- Organizations tend to shift their compliance structures from incongruent to congruent types, and resist a shift away from congruence.
- The legitimacy of power is in itself not more likely to make its use more effective. However, normative power is more likely and coercive power least likely to be seen as legitimate.
- Involvement in an organization is affected both by the legitimacy of a directive and by the degree to which it frustrates needs, wishes and desires.
- An individual's commitment to a directive is not the same as compliance. Commitment can occur when legitimate directives are in line with internalized needs of the subordinate.

Each organizational rank has its own compliance pattern. 'Lower' ranks have more complicated compliance relations than higher ranks. The lower ranks are employees, workers, members, inmates, etc. These terms are the result of lower participants' positions on three analytical dimensions:

nature of involvement, degree of subordination and performance requirement. According to Etzioni, those participants without a high position on either of these dimensions are not, in fact, within the organization's boundaries. Therefore, customers are not participants.

Based on his classification of compliance patterns, Etzioni concluded that there are three types of formal organizations: **normative organizations** which people join voluntarily because they consider the goals morally worthwhile, **utilitarian organizations** which people join in pursuit of material rewards, and **coercive organizations** which people join because they are forced to.

When to use it

There is no one right way to use this model. In a way that is objective, yet comfortable for your organization, determine which types of power are used in your organization and whether or not there is a congruent compliance relation with the involvement of the subordinates. By shifting towards more congruent compliance patterns, the organization can be more effective and efficient in its use of power. Benchmarking the process of issuing directives with other organizations, or even among different parts of an organization can be structured through the use of this model.

Lower participants	Nature of involvement	Subordination	Performance obligation
Inmates	● Negative	●	●
Employees	● Positive or negative	●	●
Customers	● Positive or negative	●	●
Parishioners	● Positive	●	●
Members	● Positive	●	●
Devoted adherents	● Positive	●	●

The final analysis

Etzioni's compliance typology helps organizations to better understand why employees are willing to follow directives or not. Also, it clearly distinguishes compliance from commitment, with which it is frequently confused.

However, many organizational scientists have argued that Etzioni's three classifications of power are too broad. In this respect, French and Raven are most often referred to. They propose five types of power:

1. referent power – based on attraction, admiration or respect;

2. expert power – the power holder has superior skills and abilities;

3. legitimate power – the power holder has been granted authority based on prevailing cultural values, accepted social structure, status or promotion within an organization;

4. reward power – subjects belief that they can be rewarded by the power holder for behaviour or performance;

5. coercive power – based on the ability to punish those who do not comply.

Core competencies

The big idea

The idea behind the 'core competencies' of an organization is to encourage managers to think inside-out as well as outside-in, the traditional approach to corporate strategic thinking. Where the outside-in approach to strategic management places the customer and the competition at the centre, core competencies refer to a combination of specific, inherent, integrated and applied knowledge, skills and attitudes of an organization that should be used as the basis for strategic intent.

In short, relatively exclusive organizational qualifications can make the difference and these should be identified and/or developed in order to create long-lasting competitive advantage.

In 1990, Hamel and Prahalad wrote an award-winning *HBR* article on the core competence of the corporation, later published a book (1994) on how to compete for the future based on the concept of the core competence. They encourage managers to ask themselves such fundamental questions as:

- What value will we deliver to our customers in, say, 10 years from now?
- What new 'competencies' (a combination of skills and technologies) will we need to develop or obtain to offer that value?
- What are the implications with regard to how we interact with our customers?

When to use it

Thinking about and trying to define core competencies for the organization stimulates management to rethink and – hopefully – mobilize the intrinsic strengths of the organization.

The future will undoubtedly bring unimaginable products, services that are simply not yet feasible and industries that don't exist today. Not only do you have to realize this, you actually need to know more or less what the future will look like. This is what Hamel and Prahalad call 'foresight'. With this foresight, the process of thinking about core competencies should help management to identify the extent to which they have or lack the chance to seize a part of that unknown future.

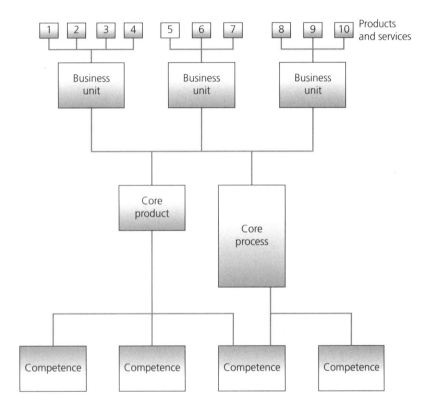

In order to develop foresight, managers need to do two things:

1. Think of the company not as a number of business units, but as a collection of core competencies.

2. Understand underlying functionalities and consider the company's performance with regard to particular processes, products and services, to logically determine what the company's unique competencies are, or should be.

For example, Volvo should not view itself as a car company, but as a company with unique competencies in product design, human safety and protection and vehicle testing.

Some tips to determine core competencies:

- Throw away your existing notion of what your company is or could be.
- Explore and cross the frontiers of your business.
- Don't be afraid to talk about things you don't understand.
- Paradoxes are good – paradigms are bad.
- Pretend you are the customer.
- Think in terms of needs, not demands.

Once management has an idea ('foresight') of what core competencies the company has or should have, it must build the **strategic architecture**. This is not a business plan, but a framework that prepares the company to (potentially) capture a large share of future revenues in emerging opportunities. The strategic architecture addresses issues and timing for what is called a broad opportunity approach:

- Which competencies must be developed?
- Which new customer groups must be understood?
- Which new channels should be pursued?
- What are the new development priorities?

The final analysis

The process of defining core competencies stimulates management to think about the company's strengths and capabilities that set it apart from the competition.

Sharply defining core competencies is so difficult that even Hamel and Prahalad sometimes seem to be unable to put their finger on it. In their zealous efforts to mention enough examples to bolster the universal application of core-competency thinking, they mix up core products and core competencies themselves. Even with the benefit of hindsight it is apparently difficult to identify core competencies, let alone come up with sharp definitions for the unknown future. Furthermore, it is obvious that core competencies are frequently not as unique and inimitable as management would like to think.

Finally, if your core competencies are hidden in the heads of people that walk away from the organization, you may want to reconsider what your core competencies really are.

Core competencies ...

The collective learning in an organization
The ability to integrate multiple skills and technologies
The capability to combine resources and knowledge to deliver superior products and services
What differentiates the organization and what makes it competitive
The very fabric of the corporation

Checklist for identification of a core competence:
■ Is it a significant source of competitive advantage?
■ Does it uniquely identify the organization?
■ Is it widespread throughout the organization?
■ Is it difficult to copy?
■ Is it difficult to put your finger on it, because it seems to be a combination of technologies, processes and the way-things-are-done in this organization?

Examples of core competencies are:
Sony – miniaturization of electronic equipment
Honda – building high-performance engines and powered vehicles
Apple – making user-friendly computer interfaces and design
Canon – integrating precision mechanics, fine optics and microelectronics
3M – relentlessly innovating adhesives and substrates.

The chicken and the egg?

Hamel and Prahalad suggest that in order to develop foresight, managers need to understand and develop their company's unique core competencies. Additionally, they must focus on underlying functionalities of their core products and services.

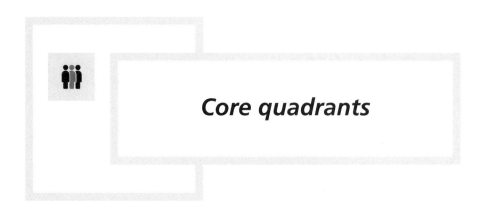

Core quadrants

The big idea

Every person has certain core qualities that truly describe the 'self'. This core quality pervades every aspect of the individual's life: words, feelings, deeds, values, etc. Stripped of all conscious and unconscious external protective and regulatory barriers of everyday life, your core quality describes 'the real you'.

What is your **core quality**? The core quadrants model by Daniel Ofman (1992, 2001) can help you determine, describe and diagnose your core quality. While it is difficult to put a finger on exactly what your core quality is, it is easier when you look at it from different perspectives:

- What is your major **pitfall** – too much of your core quality?
- What is your biggest **challenge** – the opposite of your pitfall?
- What is your **allergy** in terms of core qualities in others – the opposite of your core quality (and too much of your challenge)?

The core quadrant shows the different, yet interdependent, perspectives of your core quality. An understanding of and active consideration for these core qualities, pitfalls, challenges and allergies strongly increases efficiency and effectiveness in human interactions.

When to use it

What is your core quality? How does one determine the four elements of a core quadrant?

The power of this model is in the fact that it offers four perspectives on a 'core quality'. Still, there are subtle differences. The same core quality may have slightly different pitfalls, challenges and allergies. For each individual, it is therefore important to specify the quadrants in greater detail.

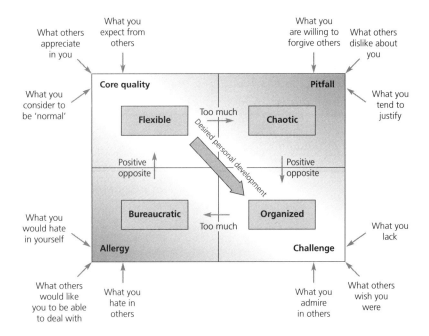

To this purpose Ofman suggests that three additional perspectives be added to each of the four elements, which can then be combined to form a personalized 'super quadrant'.

- something that **you** would say, feel, like, condone, wish, miss or hate **about yourself**;
- something that **you** would say, feel, like, condone, wish, miss or hate **about others**;
- something that **others** would say, feel, like, condone, wish, miss or hate **about you**.

The super quadrant is uncomfortably revealing: inconsistencies between the three 'super quadrant' perspectives are a relatively sure indicator that you are not who and/or how you want to be. You are, in fact, trying to hide your true feelings, avoid your pitfalls and curb your dislike of your allergy. In other words, you are 'acting'.

Incongruence in a core quadrant can also be an indicator that you might be describing the symptoms or effects of a pitfall. For example, the core quality 'enthusiasm' could lead to the pitfall fanatism, leading to negative feedback, causing disappointment, fuelling retreat, and eventually egotism. Yet, egotism itself is not the pitfall.

The core quadrants can be used to prepare for meetings where people with opposing core qualities interact. Instead of a confrontation, both parties can muster (more) respect and try to learn from each other.

The final analysis

Core quadrants have proven to be very helpful in increasing mutual understanding and respect among people with opposing core qualities. There is, however, an inherent danger in 'classifying' oneself or someone else wrongly. It is important to involve others in the perspectives.

At the end of the day, the continual effort of remaining aware of one's core quality, though difficult, is perhaps the closest approximation of being true to oneself and succeeding in life.

Covey's seven habits of highly effective people

The big idea

Wildly popular throughout the 1990s and into the 21st century, Stephen Covey (1999) has changed the face of many ambitious a manager's night-stand. He says that highly effective people have seven habits that make them very successful in life and business; furthermore, they do exactly what they feel is both right and important, and they do it consciously.

When to use it

In order to become highly effective, you should:

1. Be proactive.
2. Begin with the end in mind.
3. Put first things first.
4. Think win–win.
5. First understand, then be understood.
6. Synergize.
7. 'Sharpen the saw'.

First, says Covey, you have to break loose from being dependent upon others. How? By achieving the practice of the first three habits:

You become **proactive**. From now on, *you* take responsibility for your own behaviour. You don't blame circumstances, conditions, or – perhaps most importantly – your conditioning for your behaviour. You actively choose your response to any situation and any person. You must be pre-pared to respond in a way that you can feel proud of. Even if that requires unearthly hard work or makes you feel uncomfortable, so be it.

When, and whatever you undertake, you must visualize the result or future that you want to achieve. Covey says: you must **begin with the end in mind**. You have a clear vision of where you want to go, or you don't go there at all. You know exactly what you want to accomplish, or you choose not to accomplish it at all. You live your life and make decisions according to your deeply held beliefs, principles or fundamental truths.

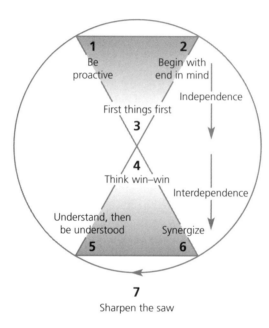

Sharpen the saw

You **put first things first**. By taking full control and staying disciplined you can focus on the most important, yet not necessarily the most urgent activities. Covey's list of such important activities includes building relationships, writing a personal mission statement, making a long-range plan, doing your workout, preparing for that presentation next week, etc. Do all those things now that would otherwise be squeezed into the last minute, delayed or even dismissed. They will help you eliminate those urgent activities that recently topped your overweight to-do list, but really were not as important. Perhaps Eisenhower's matrix will come in handy? See Eisenhower's effective time management, later in this book.

Now that you have reached the point of being independent and you are using your time to effect your most important goals in life, you must increase your effectiveness with others around you.

You need to **think win–win**. You must believe in 'abundance'; there is plenty for everyone. One person's success does not necessarily require someone else's failure. You seek solutions to problems that allow all parties involved (including yourself) to benefit.

You can make people around you feel like winners if you **understand first, then try to be understood**. You might actually learn something from them in process, now that you finally start to shut up *and* listen. In fact, you listen with the strong intent to fully, deeply understand the other person on both an intellectual analytical and emotional level. Diagnose before you prescribe, says Covey.

Finally, you need to **synergize**. This means that you open your mind to fresh, creative ideas. You become an agent of innovation, a trailblazer and a pathfinder. You are convinced that the whole is greater than the sum of its parts. You value differences between people and try to build upon those differences (see references and further reading for Belbin's team roles). You come up with a creative way out of a conflict situation.

You have now reached a stage of interdependence. You are effective and admired by family, friends and co-workers. But you should never allow yourself to rest on your laurels. You must '**sharpen the saw**', meaning that you continuously try to improve yourself. You keep innovating and refining. You have a relentless thirst for learning and exploring.

The final analysis

The issue is: what drives people to do the things they do and how do they become happy at it? Covey appeals to business managers and all other professionals who take themselves seriously by bringing it all back to one commonly understood concept: effectiveness. Effectiveness and being able to do all those important things that make us love life and others love us is the ultimate dream of the overworked manager. Whatever happened to that world trip you dreamed of 20 years ago?

Covey is right, no doubt about it. So, however, are all the others offering self-help with desired characteristics, mega-skills, principles, values and so on. Putting it into practice is the hard part. However, very few people have made it so easy to understand as Stephen Covey.

Customer marketing and relationship management

The big idea

There is more value to your customer than the current sale. If you can successfully identify your most valuable customers, acquire them, keep them, and grow their purchases, you will generate significantly more value than with one-size-fits-all approach.

Although many tools, bells and whistles are available today to implement customer marketing and relationship management, the key success behind it seems to be in giving the customer the perception that he or she is recognized promptly and serviced appropriately through multiple, integrated interfaces. This requires strategically managing all interactions with the customer through:

- customer-driven, outside-in marketing strategy;
- superior operations, systems and procedures to support the customer interface;
- customer-focused values and culture ('drive to deliver and delight').

When to use it

Putting the practice of customer marketing and customer relationship management to work is a well-discussed topic in today's professional literature. We have chosen to highlight just a few of the most basic tools available.

The **customer pyramid** can be customized based on company-specific factors to reflect how the (future) customer and potential customer base can be seen. Such factors usually include, but are not limited to turnover and profitability per customer. Different marketing tactics and tools can be applied based on this segmentation. Obviously, key customers and large potential customers get the best treatment.

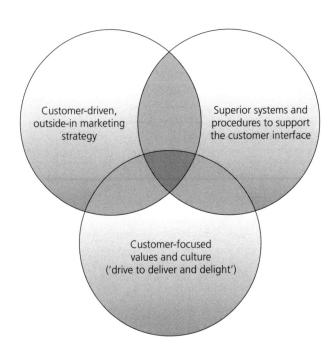

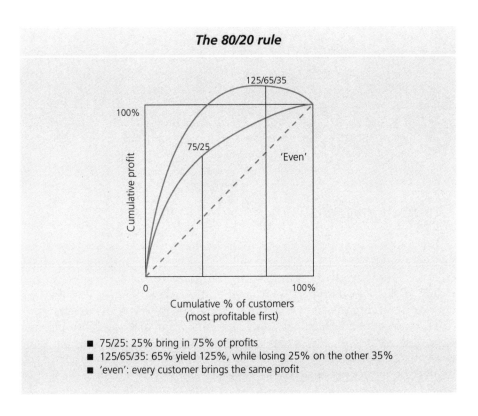

The 80/20 rule

- 75/25: 25% bring in 75% of profits
- 125/65/35: 65% yield 125%, while losing 25% on the other 35%
- 'even': every customer brings the same profit

Often used for determining which customers fall into what category is the **80/20 rule**. This popular rule says that 20 per cent of customers account for 80 per cent of the profit and the other 80 per cent only contribute the remaining 20 per cent. As a way of thinking, this is useful. Although the percentages may be different, the key idea behind this rule is that not all customers are profitable – some even cost you money!

Once you know who your most valuable (potential) customers are, the following steps should be undertaken:

- Gather as much relevant information on your (potential) customers as you can.
- Analyse this information, redesigning your information needs as you go.
- Create targets for how you want your customer to perceive you as a provider of products, services and/or experiences.
- Choose media, systems and content for your communication and interaction with your customers.
- Develop rules of engagement and 'packages' for each customer segment.
- Embed a customer-driven culture in your company.
- Store and analyse data on your customers (how, is another story!).
- Develop your customer management systems as you learn.

Compared to Henry Ford's mass-production 'only black color' model T, marketers have come a long way when it comes to differentiating products based on the needs of distinct customer groups (segments) and even individuals.

Or have they? Customer marketing and relationship management is today's high-tech, mass-scale answer to creating the same personalized, one-to-one customer interaction that was common in the local grocery store a century ago.

The final analysis

There is a plethora of models and tools available to support managers and business analysts in customer marketing and relationship management. One of the inherent dangers is the tendency to focus on getting the readily available Customer Relationship Management suites installed, as opposed to taking the time to consider the scope of potential customers.

The success of an organization in targeting, acquiring and retaining customers is, of course, also influenced by many factors besides customer relationship management. Pricing and the intrinsic value proposition of the product or service are just two examples of the various attributes that are all too easily swept under the corporate marketing header. More generic problem areas also exist, such as the lack of a wholesome marketing strategy and company culture endorsement of a customer-centric approach.

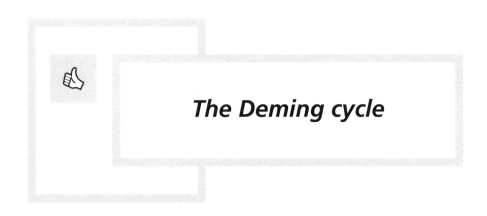

The Deming cycle

The big idea

The Deming cycle, Walton and Deming (1986), or PDSA cycle, refers to a logical sequence of four repetitive steps for continuous improvement and learning: Plan, Do, Check (also known as Study) and Act (or Action).

Planning ('Plan') the improvement of an activity should be followed by execution ('Do') of the activity according to the plan. One should then measure and study ('Check') the results and the improvement. Action ('Act') should then be taken toward adapting the objectives and/or improvement. The consequent learning should be implemented in planning the new activities.

The Deming cycle allows an organization to manage improvement initiatives in an disciplined fashion. When confronted with this model for the first time, many realize that they are steering, but not really managing their organization.

When to use it

Systematically go through the four steps when pursuing improvement in specified activities.

Plan ahead for change. Analyse the current situation and potential impacts of adjustments before doing anything else. Predict what different results are expected, with or without a theory. How can you measure the impact, if and when the desired result has been achieved? Plan to include result measurement in the execution. Make an implementation plan with assigned responsibilities for participants.

Experience shows that it doesn't hurt to ask the following questions:

- What are we trying to achieve?
- How can this be linked to the higher purpose of our organization?

- Who is/are going to be affected?
- Where will it happen?
- When will it happen?
- What is the step-by-step procedure?
- How can we measure the improvement, if at all?

When executing, **do** take small steps in controlled circumstances in order to be able to attribute improvements (or failures) to the planned changes in the activity.

Study the results of your experiment. Did the desired result occur? If not, why not?

Take **act**ion to standardize the process that produced the desired result, or, in the event that the result proved to be different from that which was desired, use the experience as input for new attempts at improvement.

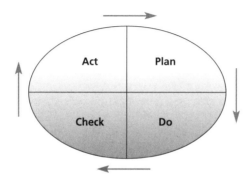

The final analysis

Many organizations are unable to specify objectives, activities and desired results, let alone to systematically and consistently manage their own improvements, Deming cycle or not.

There have been several adaptations of the Deming cycle. For example, *Plan* can be split up into: determine goals and targets, and determine methods of reaching goals. *Do* can be split up in training and education, and implementation.

The Deming cycle constitutes an important part of *kaizen* thinking described later in this book.

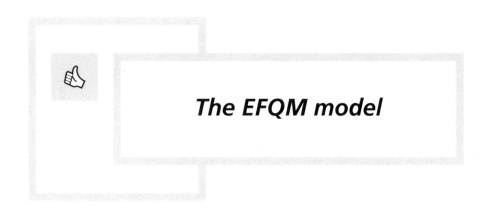

The EFQM model

The big idea

The *European Foundation for Quality Management* (EFQM) *model* helps organizations to establish an appropriate management system to set them on the path to excellence. The model explains gaps in performance and helps identify improvements. It is a non-prescriptive framework underpinned by so-called 'fundamental concepts':

- results orientation
- customer focus
- leadership and constancy of purpose
- management by processes and facts
- people development and involvement
- continuous learning, innovation and improvement
- partnership development
- public responsibility.

The EFQM model is based on the premise that excellent results with respect to performance, customers, people and society are achieved through partnerships, resources and processes.

When to use it

The model discerns five organizational areas (enablers) and four performance areas (results). The organizational areas are key elements in managing an organization: *leadership, policy and strategy, people, partnerships and resources*, and *processes*. Performance areas provide measuring indicators for the organization's fitness and achievements: customer results, people results, society results, as well as key financial results.

Leadership requires managers:

- to develop mission, vision and values;
- to be role models of a culture of excellence;
- to be personally involved in developing, implementing and improving the organization's management system;
- to be involved with customers, partners and representatives of society;
- to motivate, support and recognize people in the organization.

The following criteria determine excellence in **policy and strategy**:

- based on present and future needs and expectations of all stakeholders;
- based on information for performance measurement, research, learning and creativity related activities;
- developed, reviewed and updated continuously;
- deployed through a framework of key processes;
- communicated and implemented.

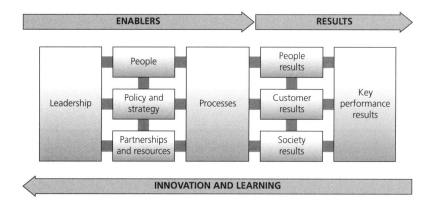

People play a key role. According to EFQM:

- Human resources should be carefully planned, managed and improved.
- People's knowledge and competencies should be identified, developed and sustained.
- People must be involved and empowered.
- There should be dialogue between people and the organization.
- People should be rewarded, recognized and cared for.

Excellency in **partnerships and resources** requires the management of:

- external partnerships
- finances
- buildings, equipment and materials
- technology
- information and knowledge.

Excellent **processes**:

- are systematically designed and managed;
- are innovatively improved to meet customer demands and increase value;
- produce well-designed and developed products and services that meet customer needs and expectations;
- produce, deliver and service products and services;
- are those that manage and enhance customer relationships.

In EFQM, **customer results**, **people results** and **society results** are measured in:

- perception measures
- performance indicators.

What the organization is achieving in relation to its planned performance are collectively called **key performance results**:

- key performance outcomes
- key performance indicators.

Additionally, a feedback loop from performance areas to create objectives in organizational areas is essential to establish a co-ordinated learning effect. Performance indicators can be generated to measure the effect of the improvements.

The final analysis

Often used by managers in Europe, the EFQM model is a recognized tool for professionalization of the planning and control cycle. The EFQM model was co-developed by top managers with such companies as Renault, Philips and Ciba Geigy. Use of the model enables core elements for managing an organization to be easily structured, analysed, assessed and improved. The EFQM website **(www.efqm.org)** is a valuable source of information on the use of the EFQM model for self-evaluation and as a benchmarking model.

The EFQM model is frequently portrayed as a model to assist with strategic decision-making. It is, however, not a prescriptive model at all, having been designed as a tool to assist with management analysis. Rather than helping to select the appropriate strategic direction, the EFQM model simply helps to realize improvements that will ultimately lead to achievement of the stated goals.

In reality, the use of the EFQM model is often limited to analysis and action, with far too little attention paid to the link between 'what we do' and 'is the result what we want?'.

Eisenhower's effective time management

The big idea

In order to be truly effective, one should always know what is important and – perhaps more importantly – what is not. Eisenhower's way to approach a full agenda and determine priorities for issues or tasks at hand discerns two dimensions:

- (relative) importance
- urgency.

Many problems related to full agendas are related to people's natural inability to discern importance from urgency. This description is our interpretation of Eisenhower's approach.

When to use it

There are five simple steps to creating your own Eisenhower matrix:

1. List.
2. Rank importance.
3. Rank urgency.
4. Plot.
5. Divide into categories.

In more detail, this is what you should do in each step:

1. List all your issues and tasks.
2. Imagine you had all the time in the world for every single item, and forget deadlines. Then rank all items (or groups) by applying an order or rank of importance.

3. Back to reality again, what is the real absolute deadline or latest possible date to start each task or to tackle each issue?

4. Plot your items on two dimensions according to their importance (see 2) and their urgency (see 3).

5. Draw dividing lines. This is where you discern priorities based on your available time or capacity.

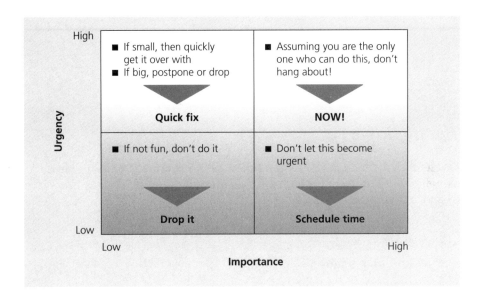

The final analysis

Effectively managing your time is only a part of being effective: you also have to do the *right* things *right*. Many people find it difficult to concentrate on things that, though important, do not have to be done *right now* (particularly when there are other things demanding attention, albeit less important ones!). The trick is to train yourself to prioritize; this way you can get all the important things (some of which may be less urgent) out of the way and thus clean up your diary.

On the whole, people are more effective when they enjoy what they are doing, and – to a limited extent – when put under pressure. Besides enjoyment and pressure, discipline has an important role to play – without it, it is impossible to make a clear distinction between high and low urgency/importance.

EVA – economic value added

The big idea

Economic value added (EVA) is a financial performance measure aimed at showing the true economic profit of an enterprise. It is an appropriate measure to use for:

- setting goals
- evaluating performance
- determining bonuses
- communicating with investors
- capital budgeting
- valuations.

Traditional accounting systems determine the value of organizations on the basis of performance measurements such as earnings per share and return on equity. However, they take no account of the effectiveness with which resources are deployed and managed, i.e. the opportunity cost of investing capital. As a result, many companies that appear profitable on paper are in fact considerably less so.

What makes EVA unique is that it focuses on measuring both value and performance. To ascertain value, subtract from the net operating profit the cost of the capital employed to generate it over a given period: EVA will show just how much wealth has been created or destroyed. To measure (and reward) performance, use increase in EVA as the measuring stick, as opposed to the attainment of budget-driven targets: pinning a bonus to the realization of a planned level of performance effectively kills any incentive to do better.

$$\text{EVA} = \begin{matrix}\text{Net Operating}\\\text{Profit after Taxes}\\\text{(NOPAT)}\end{matrix} \left[\text{Capital} \times \text{The Cost of Capital}\right]$$

When to use it

Attention must be paid to four areas for successful application:

- measurement
- management
- motivation
- mindset.

With regard to *measurement*, three steps should be taken. Firstly, establish rules to convert accounting profit to economic profit, i.e. to adjust conventional earnings to eliminate accounting anomalies affecting economic results. Next, identify EVA centres within the organization – these may be large or small, but must all be accountable for their own results. Then link these centres so as to harmonize decisions across the organization. This enables EVA to be tracked unit by unit on a monthly basis.

Measuring EVA is one thing; acting on the results is another. *Management* and EVA, therefore, must become inextricably linked. Budgeting and planning techniques must be adjusted to incorporate the concept, and a link established to operating and strategic levers. Finally, checks must be carried out to ensure that EVA-thinking actually sticks.

By basing incentive compensation on an increase in EVA, managers can be *motivated* to think and act like owners because they are paid like owners – by increasing shareholder wealth, they simultaneously increase their own. Bonuses and other incentives, therefore, must be linked to performance as opposed to budgets, allowing managers to focus on

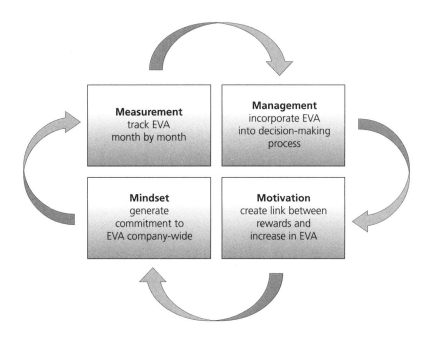

maximizing wealth instead of merely meeting corporate expectations. It goes without saying that a certain degree of risk must also be involved, with penalties for underperformance. An additional advantage is that shifting from continuous negotiation of financial targets to a one-time setting of bonus parameters greatly simplifies the planning process.

Last but not least, there is *mindset*. EVA is, in effect, an internal governance system under which individuals are automatically encouraged to work in the best interests of the shareholders. When fully implemented it has the potential to transform corporate culture. Company-wide commitment and training is essential: if EVA is not recognized as having priority, but simply added to the list of performance measurements, the result will be confusion and unnecessary complexity.

The final analysis

Despite being described as a measure of financial performance, and moreover one which can theoretically be calculated, it is important to remember that EVA is not so much about generating a specific figure as about capital growth in general.

The word 'theoretically' speaks volumes: one of the main problems in trying to calculate the true cost of capital is that you have to decide which anomalies should be included in the calculation. The very fact that there are over 150 such anomalies illustrates the impossibility of ever being able to come up with a precise figure. Stern in fact recommends selecting no more than 15, emphasizing that the intention is to take into consideration only the most important factors in an attempt to identify growth and put a rough figure on your cost of capital.

As with many models, the steps to be taken are far easier to write down than to put into practice. However, simply by stimulating managers to break out of their current mindset and think laterally a great deal can be achieved. The steps to be taken when calculating EVA should therefore be viewed not as a straitjacket, but as a list of items for consideration.

The fifth discipline

The big idea

In learning organizations, people continually expand their capacity to create desired results, as new ways of thinking are nurtured, collective ambitions prevail and people learn from each other. In his bestselling book, Peter Senge (1994) described five disciplines that together constitute the key ingredients for a learning organization:

- systems thinking
- personal mastery
- mental models
- shared vision
- team learning.

Systems thinking is what Senge calls 'the fifth discipline', because it makes the disciplines work together for the benefit of the business. It provides a way of understanding practical business issues in terms of particular cycles and levels of detail or complexity. The essence is to see interrelationships between processes, rather than status quo 'snapshots' and linear cause-and-effect chains. The key concept of systems thinking is 'feedback', which refers to how actions can cause, reinforce or counteract each other. When actions influence each other in closed loops or cycles, we speak of 'archetypes'. Generic archetypes are:

- Balancing process with delay – excessive corrective measures lead to strong ups or downs as the desired effect is delayed.
- Limits to growth – reaching a level of saturation, possibly even leading to suffocation.
- Shifting the burden – continuation of short-term measures that fight symptoms rather than the underlying problem(s).

- Shifting the burden to the interferon – becoming dependent upon outside help to fight the symptoms of the problem.
- Eroding goals – easing long-term goals as current problems take precedence.
- Escalation – an uncontrolled zero-sum game, such as price wars.
- Success to the successful – reinforcing the advantage of an initiative at the expense of support for the alternative.
- Tragedy of the commons – domino effect of exhausting common resources or target markets, leading to depletion of resources or suffocation of markets.
- Fixes that fail – 'cure worse than disease'.
- Growth and underinvestment – uncontrolled growth to keep up with demand, resulting in lower quality and lack of competitive insight.

Personal mastery refers to the ability to continue to clarify and deepen personal vision, to focus energy, to develop patience, and to see reality objectively. One important aspect of personal mastery is to utilize the so-called 'creative tension' that inherently exists between personal vision and current reality (observed objectively).

Mental models are assumptions and generalizations of how we see the world. They determine how we think we can successfully interact with the world. The discipline of working with mental models requires unearthing one's own mental models, exposing them, and opening up for alternative perspectives and insight. Key skills are:

- Recognizing 'leaps of abstraction' – realizing that one often jumps from observations to generalizations.
- Exposing the 'left-hand column' – articulating our conscious or unconscious thoughts when we communicate, exposing distortions or even contradictions between what we think and what we say.
- Balancing inquiry and advocacy – putting emphasis on listening and observing, as well as speaking and controlling.
- Distinguishing between espoused theories (said) and implicit theories (done).

Shared visions emerge from personal visions, deriving energy and fostering commitment as they evolve. The more people share the vision or enrol in it, the more likely they feel it is achievable. People will start working towards the vision. Compliance is often mistaken for enrolment or commitment to a vision – many managers find themselves left in the cold, feeling betrayed when the going gets tough, because though seemed everyone was aboard, they were in fact only complying.

Team learning requires the discipline of suspending personal assumptions and thinking together, of learning how to recognize patterns of interaction and how they may both undermine and enhance learning. One must understand the fundamental difference between dialogue and discussion. In a dialogue, there is a free and creative exploration of

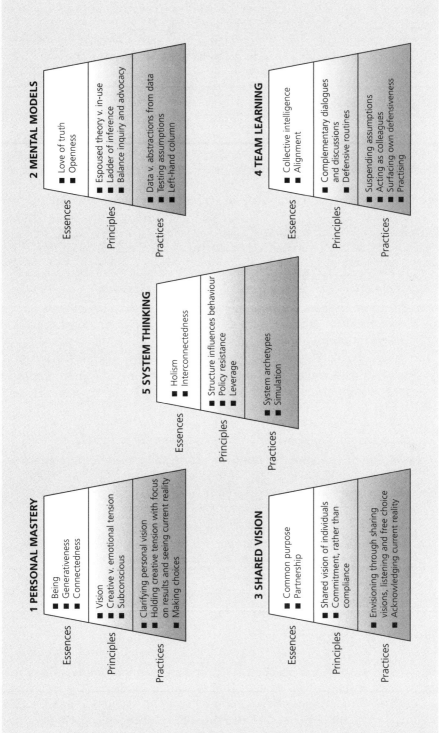

2 MENTAL MODELS

Essences
- Love of truth
- Openness

Principles
- Espoused theory v. in-use
- Ladder of inference
- Balance inquiry and advocacy

Practices
- Data v. abstractions from data
- Testing assumptions
- Left-hand column

4 TEAM LEARNING

Essences
- Collective intelligence
- Alignment

Principles
- Complementary dialogues and discussions
- Defensive routines

Practices
- Suspending assumptions
- Acting as colleagues
- Surfacing own defensiveness
- Practising

5 SYSTEM THINKING

Essences
- Holism
- Interconnectedness

Principles
- Structure influences behaviour
- Policy resistance
- Leverage

Practices
- System archetypes
- Simulation

1 PERSONAL MASTERY

Essences
- Being
- Generativeness
- Connectedness

Principles
- Vision
- Creative v. emotional tension
- Subconscious

Practices
- Clarifying personal vision
- Holding creative tension with focus on results and seeing current reality
- Making choices

3 SHARED VISION

Essences
- Common purpose
- Partnership

Principles
- Shared vision of individuals
- Commitment, rather than compliance

Practices
- Envisioning through sharing visions, listening and free choice
- Acknowledging current reality

complex and subtle issues. By contrast, a discussion is characterized by the presentation and defence of different perspectives and opinions in search of the best answer to a problem.

Senge stresses that dialogue and discussion are potentially complementary, but most teams lack the ability to distinguish between the two.

When to use it

Each discipline has both different aspects (business, personal, interpersonal) and levels (practice, principle, essence). As a result, using the disciplines is difficult or, more romantically put by Senge *et al.*, 'a life-long effort'. Both enthusiasts and critics have requested tips for putting the 'universal truth' of the 'fifth discipline' into practice. We refer to the Fieldbook and the Dance of Change book for more detailed self-help tips for managers.

In short, the key ideas behind practising the five disciplines are:

- **Systems thinking** all comes down to finding the point in the cycle where efforts to effectuate change are most effective.
- **Personal mastery** means that you should be true to yourself. Meditation for self-discovery and consciousness is key to successful pursuit of personal mastery.
- Tools for uprooting your paradigmatic, preconceived notions of the world and expose **mental models** suggested by Senge are: mental mapping (personal level), honing listening skills (interpersonal) and scenario planning (business level). Perhaps you are too high up the ladder of inference, taking actions based on beliefs rather than observing and experiencing on the other end of the ladder?
- Enrolment in a **shared vision** results from free choice and genuine enthusiasm for a vision. Individuals trying to get buy-in for their vision should believe in themselves, understand the vision (what, why and how), refrain from overselling and ignoring genuine concerns, and let people choose for themselves.
- **Team learning** can be stimulated through sessions with a managed balance between dialogue and discussion. Explicit mapping of mental models and assumptions, as well as methods to make people willing to speak out and suspend their assumptions are key.

The final analysis

Senge is right. But putting the fifth discipline into practice is a daunting task that may take longer than anyone is willing to commit to. The learning organization is very abstract and also sort of a 'catch-all,' affecting an organization at all levels and in all functions. Additionally, there is a very real chance that politics may hinder learning.

Four competencies of the learning organization

The big idea

Knowledge is the key concept in developing a learning organization, even more so as organizations have become increasingly knowledge intensive. Sprenger and ten Have (1996) say that successful knowledge management requires four learning competencies to manage the knowledge flow in an organization:

- **absorption** of knowledge from outside
- **diffusion** of knowledge within
- **generation** of knowledge within
- **exploitation** of knowledge in products and services.

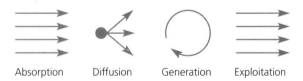

Four competencies of the learning organization

Absorption   Diffusion   Generation   Exploitation

Rather than knowledge itself, argue Sprenger and ten Have, it is the combined ability of an organization to absorb, diffuse, generate and exploit it that secures true competitive advantage. In fact, there is a profound difference between the 'profile' approach and the 'competency' approach to creating a learning organization.

Different approaches to organizational learning

Profile approach	Competency approach
■ Redesign ■ Benchmarking best practice	■ Based on creating skills and harbouring resources for sustained learning
■ Clear vision for management based on blueprint	■ No blueprint ■ People devise improvements and learn naturally
■ Profile not conducive to creativity and initiative	■ Learning competancies require continuous commitment to organizational learning and change

The profile approach attempts to create both a new organizational structure and systems to enable learning processes. This, however, is conducive of 'consumptive' behaviour, as opposed to learning behaviour. A competency approach to organizational learning is much more sustainable.

When to use it

There is no such thing as a bad time to enhance organizational learning. More often than not, though, managers are directly confronted with the need to critically assess the learning ability of their organizations. Some clear indicators of this need are:

- poor problem solving, reinventing the wheel
- failing innovation processes
- frequent budget overruns
- sense of inability to deliver
- no measurable effect of formal education.

The first step in enhancing organizational learning is to create understanding and awareness of organizational learning. A diagnosis of the organization's learning ability increases such understanding and awareness. Furthermore, the diagnosis itself effectively creates a foundation for action.

It is important to understand why knowledge is so important, but also what the different types of knowledge are, where knowledge is stored, and how it flows (or not) through the organization.

The four types of knowledge are (Dierk 1994):

- subject or expert knowledge on a particular industry or discipline;
- methodological knowledge on how to approach types of problems or projects;

- social knowledge to understand human interaction and to facilitate communicative processes, particularly the exchange of knowledge;
- 'know-how' to put knowledge into action, based on practice and experience.

Knowledge is stored in four ways (Quinn 1992):

- in people's heads, from formal education, experience, information exchange, etc.;
- in technical systems through years of data gathering, analysis, coding, restructuring and redesign. Some examples are manuals, work procedures and database structures;
- in management systems, both formal and informal, such as in meeting rules, management styles, project management, quality control and information management;
- in norms and values, to keep the above together, such as a shared understanding of how learning should occur, as well as openness, curiosity, and how to deal with conflicts of interests.

The second step in using this model is a diagnosis of the learning ability of the organization along the balancing scales of the four learning competencies.

Instruments for growing organizational learning competencies

Absorption	Diffusion	Generation	Exploitation
■ External professional networks ■ Education ■ Conferences ■ Customer contacts ■ Competitive analysis ■ Supplier co-operation ■ Acquisition ■ Patents and licences ■ Research ■ Knowledge management ■ Creative scenarios	■ Assembly and use of manuals ■ Regulations and procedures ■ Knowledge information systems ■ Best practice study ■ Internal knowledge exchange ■ Coaching and mentoring ■ Peer assessment ■ Informal networks ■ Job rotation	■ Programme and project management ■ Concepts of final reports and products ■ Simulation of markets and processes ■ Quality reviews ■ Action learning ■ Dialogue ■ Self assessment ■ Performance measurement and rewards ■ Business process reengineering ■ Professional feedback	■ Cross-disciplinary project teams ■ Using existing know-how for new products ■ Market research ■ Promoting knowledge (internally and externally) ■ Improving products based on customer reviews ■ Prototyping ■ Delivery ■ Breaking through learning barriers

The diagnosis should address these issues:

- What instruments are available and which of these are used?
- How does management direct learning?
- What is the balance between knowledge in people and knowledge in systems?
- Which are the learning obstacles?

The third step is to connect the key issues emerging from the diagnosis with (corrective) measures. For this process, Sprenger and ten Have propose five steps:

1. Analyse and discuss issues and obstacles.
2. Gain insight as to the cause of problems among the organisation's members in decreasing levels of abstraction.
3. Formulate learning objectives and a knowledge management policy.
4. Focus on solutions to learning obstacles.
5. Implement learning instruments.

The instruments to increase organizational learning can also be used as a checklist in interviews with management and operational groups to answer some of the key questions in the diagnosis.

The final analysis

The strength of this model is in the concept of organizational learning through the identification and stimulation of learning competencies, as opposed to creating a blueprint or redesigning the organization in an image.

The model offers a transparent set of concepts to help create a learning organization. On the other hand, there is little focus on the so-called mental models, which are often hot topics in organizational learning. How to deal with organizational power play and politics is left untouched.

The model proposes a learning competency associated with each of the four knowledge flows identified by the authors. However, when knowledge management is approached from a systems perspective, the analogy can be taken even further. The productive use of knowledge is not the only way in which knowledge 'flows' out. Knowledge can also be used inappropriately, can be of inferior quality, or simply be wrong. Finally, knowledge can also flow out of the organization, as (disgruntled) people leave and (misunderstood) systems are replaced.

Safeguards against poor knowledge and/or its inappropriate use, as well as against the 'drain' of knowledge support the argument for a competency approach. Similar reasoning can be applied to devise alternative ways in which knowledge enters an organization.

Learning competencies blanced between people and systems

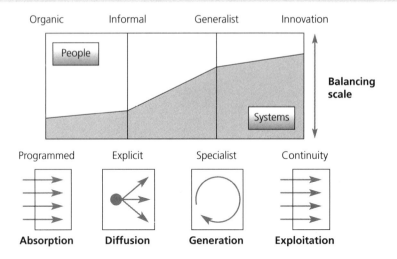

Organic Informal Generalist Innovation

People

Systems

Balancing
scale

Programmed Explicit Specialist Continuity

Absorption **Diffusion** **Generation** **Exploitation**

Generic competitive strategies

The big idea

According to Michael Porter (1979, 1980), competitive strategy is about taking offensive or defensive action to create a defendable position in an industry, in order to cope successfully with competitive forces and generate a superior return on investment. In fact, says Porter, there are only three internally consistent and successful strategies for outperforming others:

1. cost leadership
2. differentiation
3. focus.

A **cost leadership** position defends an organization against all five competitive forces:

- *competitive rivalry*: low cost means more margin to squeeze in a battle for the lowest price;
- *buyers' negotiation power*: prices can only be lower at even more efficient competitors;
- *supplier power*: more margin to cope with price increases;
- *new entrants*: it is harder to compete with existing, efficient players;
- *substitution*: favourable position relative to competitors usually obtained quickly.

An alternative to cost leadership, **differentiation**, is to worry less about costs, but instead to seek to be perceived as offering something that nobody else can offer. Be it durable, novel, rare, serviced globally, very reliable or of high emotional value, differentiation requires the product to appeal to customers in other ways than low price. Differentiators have to invest more in research, design, materials, service, etc.

There can be only one cost leader in any industry, yet there can be multiple differentiators: cost has only one dimension, while differentiation can be done in many ways. Logically, one can conclude that one has to choose. This choice depends on a company's ability to deliver and compete, even if it can't compete for all customers. In fact, argues Porter, companies may choose to **focus** on only a particular group of customers within a market or a limited product line. The focus strategy is built around serving a specific (narrow) market segment extremely well. Porter adds to this that within a particular focus market (often referred to as a niche), cost leadership and differentiation are options.

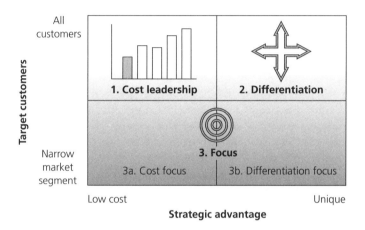

Porter's conclusion is that a company has no option but to choose one of the three generic strategies, or risk getting 'stuck in the middle'. By logical deduction, this is undesirable because there will inevitably be a competitor that is either cheaper or better differentiated than your company is.

When to use it

All you have to do is determine where your company and/or its products are (or should be in the matrix); as with many things, this is undoubtedly easier said than done! Honesty is essential, as is the need to look objectively at your own organization and the products you offer from the customer's point of view. Asking yourself the following questions can help:

- What is/can be different about what we offer as opposed to the offerings of our competitors (and how can this be exploited)?
- Do these differences represent superior value to some/all of the customers in this market (if the answer is no, you clearly have a problem!)?
- Are these differences sustainable and defendable?

Having established your current position, appropriate steps can then be taken to either maintain or improve it – at this point think about the difference between where your organization and its products are now, in relation to where you would ideally like them to be.

The final analysis

Plotting your company and its competitors on a generic competitive strategy chart or matrix is a very useful exercise early in the strategy process. The problem is: how to measure your company's relative position?

The main difficulty with regard to determining cost leadership lies in the lack of transparency as regards the actual costs of competitors; it is difficult enough to calculate actual costs within your company. Assessing (the extent of) differentiation and the extent to which customers *appreciate* the differentiated proposition is trickier still.

There are various ways in which one can try to overcome these obstacles for using the concept of the generic competitive strategies. Indicators for cost leadership *could* be the price of a company's product, the size of the company, its strategic partnerships with, or even ownership of, suppliers and distributors, labour costs, etc.

Differentiation can be obvious, yet harder to measure. By that, we mean that a BMW is differentiated in terms of prestige and image, but so is a Mercedes. How much more or less is one differentiated from the other? What about subtle nuances? Both brands of automobiles have a differentiated focus (3b), but what makes customers choose one above the other?

Happily stuck in the middle

Although Porter, with his competitive forces analysis, generic strategies and value chain, has taken a lot of the guesswork out of strategic planning and replaced it with internally consistent and seemingly logical trade-offs, many companies nonetheless managed to get themselves happily stuck in the doomed middle. These companies (e.g. Wal-Mart, Toyota) were once differentiated cost leaders.

In 1994, Henry Mintzberg wrote an influential *HBR* article, 'The Rise and Fall of Strategic Planning', in which he summed up the problems with rigid strategic planning as preached by Michael Porter and others. Strategic planning is an analytical process that obstructs strategic thinking: A creative and intuitive process of synthesizing an integrated perspective of the company. Things change while you are busy planning. Data required for analysis not only takes long enough to harden to be outdated by the time it is integrated in the strategic plan, it also tends not to contain the critical nuances of some of the soft data. Also, said Mintzberg, strategy cannot be formalized; the assumption that plans follow a rational and orderly sequence does not hold. Mintzberg correctly noticed that, sometimes, acting goes before thinking – and some companies thrive on it.

To make full use of Porter's generic competitive strategies, other tools and models are also required, for example, cost price analyses, competitive differentiation analyses, competitive forces analyses and the value chain analysis.

The gods of management

The big idea

Charles Handy (1978–1995) uses four Greek gods to illustrate four more or less generic management styles and their resulting organizational structures. Each god, or company culture, is based on a set of key assumptions held by its members about power, influence, motivation, learning and how changes occur.

The four gods are:

Zeus – one strong charismatic leader. The power and influence of individuals in the *club*, or 'gang' if you will, is wholly dependent on their relationship with the leader. Good examples are young entrepreneurial organizations, political groups and specialized professional service firms. Street gangs and criminal organizations also fit this profile.

Apollo – highly structured and stable: all members know their *roles* and positions in the hierarchy. Many rules and regulations govern the way people work and interact. This is your typical bureaucracy, such as a 100-year-old insurance corporation or bank.

Athena – all about talent, energy, and ambition. Individuals are recognized and rewarded in accordance with well they perform their *tasks* in teams. This type of organization is common among consulting firms, advertising agencies, research companies and business units of high-tech enterprises.

Dionysus – serves mainly as an infrastructure for the *existence* and pursuit of purpose of its individual members. Good examples are universities, group medical practices, and lawyers sharing office space and secretarial services.

The god	The Culture	Thinking and learning	Influencing and changing	Motivating and rewarding
Zeus	Club	■ Intuitive, holistic ■ Trial-and-error ■ Decisions based on 'soft' data ■ Synthesizing	■ Personal charisma and reputation ■ Control of resources ■ Replace weak links	■ Seeking power and discretion over people and events ■ Money as a symbol or enabler
Apollo	Role	■ Logical, sequential and analytical ■ Training ('on the job') ■ Transfer of data and information	■ Authority based on position, role or title ■ Change requires roles and rules to change	■ Order and predictability ■ Formal contracts and remuneration
Athena	Task	■ Problem solvers ■ Team analysis ■ Logic and creativity ■ Continual discovery	■ Wisdom and expertise earn respect ■ Persuasion ■ Agreement ■ 'Boxing' the problem	■ Exposure to variety ■ Trusted in and discretion over problem approach ■ Self-advancement
Dionysus	Existential	■ Detest classification ■ Learn by immersion and new experiences	■ Hard to influence ■ One-on-one management	■ Personal freedom above all

Hardy argues that a mismatch between the organization's culture and how members act according to their 'gods' will negatively impact the effectiveness of the organization and of its members. So-called cultural confusion will show up in inefficiency and slack: unused resources, longer-than-necessary lead-times, increased overtime, overstaffing. Hardy calls slack the organizational balm to ease the pain of inefficiency: a quick fix, but not a solution.

When to use it

Hardy uses this model to help managers address inefficiency problems from an organizational culture perspective. The major cultural crises that affect today's organizations are rooted in the misappropriation of efficiency efforts, to the point where this has reached a 'dead end'. Organizations eventually become paralyzed by their multiple Apollonian layers and structures. Inflexibility and the increased risk of employing people adhering to different 'gods of management' in such big organizations lead to conflicts and inefficiency. For organizational efficiency, it is essential that there is cultural purity. Harmony is health.

At the same time, organizations ought to live with, even cherish, the diversity of gods. After all, says Hardy, organizations are just large sets of diverse jobs to be done. The three categories of jobs are:

- steady-state (Apollo is the god)
- development (Athena is the goddess)
- Asterix situations, requiring intuition and instinct (Zeus and Dionysus are the gods).

Management is the act of reconciling these different 'divine organizational forces'. Hardy's model may help in determining how to manage these forces. In order to do this, one must realize that countervailing forces are different in each organization, depending on the principle force's size, life cycles, work patterns and people.

Once the **size** of an organization reaches a point where individuals can no longer be aware of each member's personality, talents and skills, the organization becomes an Apollo.

A shorter **life cycle**, or higher rate of change, is an indicator of the extent to which Athena is at work in an organization. The problem-solving capacity can be increased by pulling people out of production into product development teams, or out of sales into market development. In this respect, decreasing administrative tasks and bringing in consultants are nothing but divine interventions by Athena.

Work patterns can be either flows (input for next step, e.g. assembly line), copies (identical work, e.g. cash registers) or units (independent work, e.g. craftsman's work). Flow and copy patterns tend to require Apollo cultures, whereas unit patterns can be Zeus-like, Athenian or

Dionysian. A change in work patterns as a result of a corporate merger can have a disastrous effect on people's work motivation.

Finally, says Hardy, there is a bit of each god in all of us. We **people** are adaptable functions of the different divine forces. Education and upbringing have a large impact on us. With the theoretical foundation of Hardy's model, an understanding of the different forces that drive people, we can assess and perhaps even influence the balance, or link the gods. This may happen through increased cultural tolerance, speaking a common language and creating 'bridges' (cross-cultural co-ordination mechanisms). Using top management as a bridge is distorting and undue use of executive time. A matrix organization is the ultimate 'bridged' organization. Formal co-ordination can be achieved through functional grouping, centralized information and individual liaisons.

The final analysis

Hardy's *Gods of Management* is a very entertaining account of how organizational cultures can make, break or bend an organization. Its primary use is in helping to understand, and perhaps decrease the organizational 'slack' that results from an organizational 'coming of age'.

It is very important to keep in mind that these are generic types of organizational cultures. Who knows? Perhaps your sales organization has an opportunistic touch of Artemis that the Hephaesti in production can't stand. And Hermes may influence your organization with a continuous process of fuelling and draining of organizational knowledge, as people enter and leave at an increasingly higher rate.

Just as the ancient Greeks knew that one should always be fearful of the 'unknown' god, we must never assume that we can fully understand the organization with this model of four generic divine forces alone.

Greiner's growth model

The big idea

Companies go through phases of growth as well as periods of stagnation, or even decline in times of crisis. The influence of time on past decisions is a major factor causing phases of evolution and revolution as organizations grow. Many of the major problems of growing companies are, in fact, rooted in solutions to old problems.

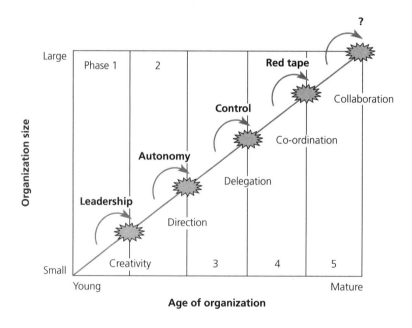

The key dimensions of Greiner's (1998) model are:

- **Age of the organization.** Management principles and problems are rooted in time, changing over the life span of an organization. Time itself is a contributing factor to the need for a revolution, as attitude and behaviour tend to become more rigid as time goes by.
- **Size of the organization.** As organizations grow, increasing numbers of people and resources must interact, levels of hierarchy increase and co-ordination becomes complex.
- **Stage of evolution.** Periods of continuous growth without major setbacks can occur, in which many organizations can successfully depend upon tried measures to problems.
- **Stages of revolution.** When 'proven' ways of doing business no longer seem to be sustainable, a revolution may occur. Some companies don't make it through such critical times and fold or sell up.
- **Industry growth rate.** A factor influencing how quickly a company goes through the various phases of [r]evolution is the industry growth rate. Evolution can be prolonged as long as profits hold up, even whilst problems are mounting in the organization. On a larger scale, a quickly developing industry will 'age' an organization faster.

Based on these key dimensions, Greiner developed a model with five generic growth phases. Most important in this model is that each phase constitutes a logical result of the preceding phase.

Phase 1 is a phase of **creativity**. The start-up company is developing both a product and a market. Characteristics of this stage are:

- technically and/or entrepreneurially oriented founders in charge with a focus on making the product and selling it;
- frequent and informal communication;
- hard work, poor pay, and perhaps of a piece of the action in the future.

As the company 'gets going', complexity comes with growth and soon the founders are struggling with the burden of managing the company, instead of running it. Conflicts become more frequent. Partners argue over new products and markets. Through lack of decisive direction, the company enters a **leadership crisis**. With the installation of a business manager, the company enters the next phase. The founders either become directors, sell up, or share ownership in order to offer incentives to new management talent. If all this happens in relative harmony, the founders take chief technology, new business, new product or new market development positions.

In **phase 2: direction**, the company enters a new period of sustained growth. The characteristics of the company have changed:

- functional organization structure
- accounting and capital management

- incentives, budgets and work standards
- more formal communication and hierarchy
- directive top management.

The directive management style funnels energy efficiently into growth. However, as the organization grows even more complex, top management is no longer able to oversee all operations and lower-level management feels tied down, despite their greater knowledge of markets and products. The **autonomy crisis** is born. Very soon, the company needs to allow decisions to be made by local and lower management, or people might leave the organization.

When entering **phase 3: delegation**, the company has implemented a decentralized organizational structure, depicted by:

- operation and market level responsibility
- profit centres and financial incentives
- decision-making based on periodic reviews
- top management acting by exception
- rare and formal corporate communication, supplemented by 'field visits'.

When to use it

Once again, the organization embarks on a period of relative prosperity, until top executives feel a loss of control. Managers abroad and in the field are acting ever more independently, running their own campaigns. As Greiner effectively puts it, freedom breeds a parochial attitude. Sooner or later, the corporation finds itself in the midst of a **control crisis**. Top management's attempts to regain control usually drown in the vast scope of operations and markets. The solution is in finding ways to co-ordinate, rather than control.

Those companies that survive the control crisis as a single entity will have found and implemented the techniques of **phase 4: co-ordination**:

- merging of local units into product groups
- thorough review of formal planning
- supervision of co-ordination by corporate staff
- centralization of support functions
- corporate scrutiny of capital expenditures
- accountability for return on investment at product group level
- motivation through lower-level profit sharing.

As limited resources are used more efficiently and local management looks beyond their own needs, the organization grows again. Product group managers have learned to justify and account for their decisions and get rewarded accordingly. Over time, however, the watchdog mentality begins to take its toll on the level of confidence that middle and lower management have in the co-ordination mechanism. Eventually, the rules and procedures become a goal instead of a means. The corporation is getting stuck in a **red tape crisis**. The organization desperately needs to increase its market agility and people need more flexibility.

In **phase 5: collaboration**, a new evolutionary path is characterized by:

- team action for problem solving
- cross-functional task teams
- decentralizations of support staff to consult to specific task teams
- matrix-type organization structure
- simplification of control mechanisms
- team behaviour education programmes
- real-time information systems
- team incentives.

In his original article, Greiner (1972) indicated having only a 'hunch' of what the next revolutionary phase would be. Psychological saturation as a crisis and dual organization structures as an evolving phase, with individuals switching on and off active ('habit structure') and passive ('reflective structure') roles to alleviate the pressure on the individual were his best guess. More recently, he has argued that perhaps, in realization of the limits to internal growth, a sixth phase would showcase an increased focus on extra-organizational solutions, such as mergers, creating holdings and managing the network of companies around the corporation.

Greiner's growth model is a descriptive model, helping companies to understand why certain management styles, organizational structures and co-ordination mechanisms work better or worse at different phases in the development of a company. Guidelines for using this model are:

- knowing where your organization stands
- recognizing your (limited) options
- realizing that solutions may breed future problems.

The final analysis

First published in 1972, Larry Greiner's growth model is still very helpful in understanding growth-related problems and the impact of their solutions on an organization. There is, however, a clear danger of typifying an organization to the point where solutions are taken for granted. One must understand that this model should be used to understand the state of the company, rather than to decide which solutions are best.

Hofstede's cultural dimensions

The big idea

In 1966, Geert Hofstede undertook what would become recognized as the most authoritative research initiative on the subject of national cultural differences. About 116,000 employees at all levels of a major multinational corporation across 50 countries were involved. All respondents were carefully matched for other characteristics, such as age, sex, and job category. The result was a massive quantity of data from which Hofstede (1981) eventually derived the conclusion that there are five major dimensions that can describe a national culture:

- power distance
- uncertainty avoidance
- individualism versus collectivism
- masculinity versus femininity
- confucian dynamism.

When to use it

When initiating international ventures within your company, or when dealing with alien business partners, customers and suppliers, Hofstede's cultural dimensions can help to prevent cultural misunderstandings and failures.

When confronted with a different national culture within or between companies, use Hofstede's five cultural dimensions to understand why the 'other party' might act differently from what you might expect, and vice versa:

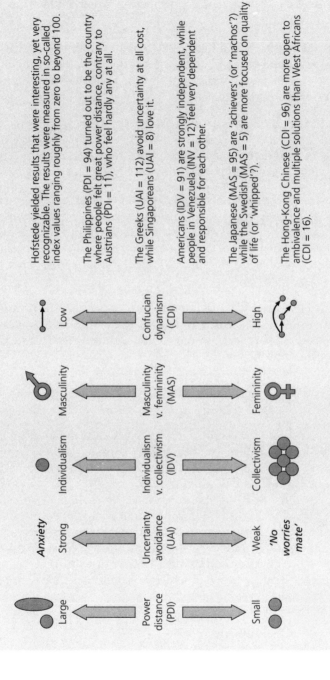

Hofstede yielded results that were interesting, yet very recognizable. The results were measured in so-called index values ranging roughly from zero to beyond 100.

The Philippines (PDI = 94) turned out to be the country where people felt great power distance, contrary to Austrians (PDI = 11), who feel hardly any at all.

The Greeks (UAI = 112) avoid uncertainty at all cost, while Singaporeans (UAI = 8) love it.

Americans (IDV = 91) are strongly independent, while people in Venezuela (INV = 12) feel very dependent and responsible for each other.

The Japanese (MAS = 95) are 'achievers' (or 'machos'?) while the Swedish (MAS = 5) are more focused on quality of life (or 'whipped'?).

The Hong-Kong Chinese (CDI = 96) are more open to ambivalence and multiple solutions than West Africans (CDI = 16).

Low ← Confucian dynamism (CDI) → High

Masculinity ← Masculinity v. femininity (MAS) → Femininity

Individualism ← Individualism v. collectivism (IDV) → Collectivism

Anxiety
Strong ← Uncertainty avoidance (UAI) → Weak
'No worries mate'

Large ← Power distance (PDI) → Small

Power distance, on a continuum between two extremes, indicates the extent to which (it is accepted that) power is distributed unequally among individuals.

The extent to which one feels threatened by ambiguous situations and tries to avoid them by living according to rules, believing in absolute truths, and avoiding conflicts is called the **uncertainty avoidance** dimension.

The **individualism versus collectivism** dimension refers to how much people feel they are supposed to either take care of or be cared for by themselves and their immediate families, as opposed to being part of a larger group with a tight social framework to which they belong.

Masculinity versus femininity is a dimension referring to the dominance of assertiveness and acquisition of things (labelled 'masculine') versus concern for people, feelings and the quality of life ('feminine'). The poles of the dimension were so labelled because men and women tend to display these respective characteristics across nearly all cultures.

Hofstede later added the last dimension, **confucian dynamism**, which refers to the extent to which a society exhibits a pragmatic future-oriented perspective rather than a conventional historic or short-term point of view.

The final analysis

Hofstede's cultural dimensions form a general introduction to, and guide-line for, dealing with foreign cultures. Of course, no two individuals are exactly alike and people may not necessarily act according to their nation's rating on Hofstede's dimensions.

One could put question marks against the ratings of some countries depending on whether all cultural groups within a country are repre-sented or not. In either case, ratings on dimensions may be very different for different people from within the same country. What about a Mexican American, or a Turkish Dutchman? Consequently, many people argue that the actual ratings (some of which are illustrated here) are subject to change as cultures develop and nations undergo demographic changes, for instance, as a result of migration.

Just-in-time

The big idea

Just-in-time (JIT) is derived from a Japanese production organization philosophy, in which inventories are seen as a bad excuse for poor planning, inflexibility, wrong machinery, quality flaws, etc. In other words, inventory represents inefficiency. The aim of JIT is to speed up customer response, while minimizing inventories.

Although inventories may secure quick response times through off-the-shelf availability, costs for such inventories may be too high. Also, low inventories increase the transparency of the production and distribution process. Especially in cases of rapidly changing specifications, complexity and high unit costs, JIT may be more effective and more efficient.

When to use it

Implementation of JIT draws close attention to the following areas:

- inventory reduction
- smaller production lot and batch sizes
- quality control
- complexity reduction and transparency
- flatter organization structure and delegation
- waste minimization.

The following techniques are at the disposal of management as regards the implementation of JIT:

- analysis of logistical parameters
- JIT simulation

- workflow analyses
- material flow analyses
- information flow analyses
- production flexibility analysis (e.g. SMED[1])
- task analysis
- pull control systems at production level (e.g. Kanban[2]).

Since the 1980s, improvements as a result of JIT measured at American and European companies have been significant. Berenschot research in 1990 showed that JIT yielded the following percentage improvements:

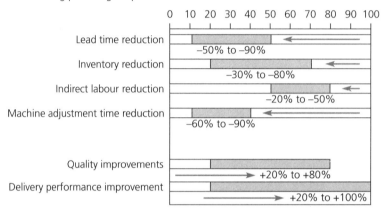

It all seems so easy! However, in order to successfully implement JIT, there are various issues and elements that must be considered in turn (in the following order):

- What results do we really want from JIT? Is it worthwhile in view of the costs and obstacles of implementation? Conduct a quick scan of costs and benefits, including a possible project planning.

[1]SMED – Single minute exchange of dye. Originating in Japan, SMED is a method of reducing change over time, whereby activities needed to produce new products are either eliminated (where possible), or carried out parallel to the production process.

[2]Kanban – a Japanese planning technique based on the principle that components should not be manufactured until they are needed, the ultimate aim being tighter control of inventories. At each stage in the production process, a container holding the components required for the manufacture of the product in question is withdrawn from the store in exchange for a card (*kanban* = Japanese for card). Only when in possession of such a card is the store authorized to replace the container. The assembly schedule then 'pulls' production through the system.

- The order of implementation of JIT is of critical importance. Lowering inventories before creating flexibility in production can lead to lousy delivery performance. Generally, our clients have been most successful implementing first at the very end of their production process and gradually working upstream, but the 'best' order of implementation depends on the situation. Increasing inventory levels temporarily should be considered so as to ensure delivery performance during the implementation.

- Certainly don't start with forcing suppliers to adopt JIT until implementation is well under way or completed.

- Does the product design qualify for JIT? Are alterations necessary? If so, do it now.

- Next, redesign the production process to enable JIT. More often than not, significant improvements and efficiencies can be obtained in this stage.

- Adjust information systems to meet demands of the primary process.

- Seek improvements with suppliers and customers. This should yield the final significant results of JIT.

The JIT game

In an effort to increase the success rate of JIT implementation, Berenschot consultants have often made use of the JIT simulation management game. This game, for groups of approximately 12 people, includes the use of simple materials, an assembly and materials handling simulation and paperwork for information flow simulation. Depending on specific needs, the game can be focused on:

- lead time reduction
- lay-out improvement
- production lot size
- reducing safety stock
- using kanban cards
- impact on machine adjustment times
- improving production organization structure
- impact of centralized planning and co-ordination

The JIT game can be played in several stages of a JIT project. Game participants contribute to an interactive process, at the same time increasing insight and improving the decision-making process.

The final analysis

JIT is especially useful in high-value production environments with a high degree of transparency in the supply chain. Communication and co-ordination with suppliers and customers is of crucial importance.

JIT production organizations are sensitive to information flaws in supply and demand. Minor disruptions in supply, production and demand can have a major negative impact on the organization's ability to deliver, as buffers are minimized.

Although JIT dates back to the 1970s in Toyota's production halls, JIT is the way of the future. Increased demand for customized products, as well as growing awareness of the cash value of inventory on the one hand, and increasing availability and use of information and communication technology on the other will further propel JIT into the 21st century.

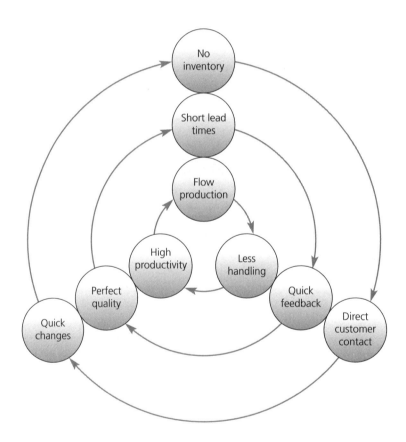

Kaizen

The big idea

Kaizen literally means change (*kai*) to become good (*zen*). Key elements of kaizen are: quality, effort, willingness to change and communication. The kaizen attitude supports a continuous process of incremental improvements within an organization.

The foundation of the kaizen model consists of five **founding elements**:

- teamwork
- personal discipline
- improved morale
- quality circles
- suggestions for improvement.

From this foundation, three key aspects of kaizen arise: elimination of *muda* (waste, inefficiency), the five-S framework for good housekeeping and standardization.

Through its impact on multiple functional parts of the organization, kaizen can eventually lead to sustainable profit management.

When to use it

First, the organization must reduce and **eliminate *muda*** (waste, inefficiency) on the production floor as a result of overproduction, excess inventory, rejected products, movement, production and assembly, waiting, transportation, etc.

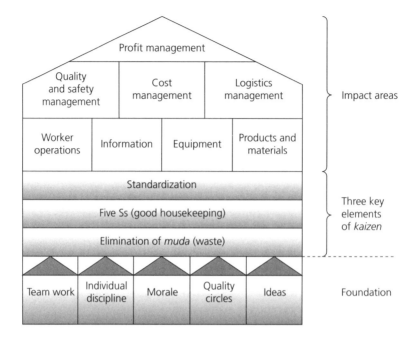

Good **housekeeping** is the next building block. This is achieved through the five Ss:

- *Seiri* – tidiness. Separate what is necessary for the work from what is not. This should help to simplify work.

- *Seiton* – orderliness. You can increase efficiency by making deliberate decisions with regard to the allocation of materials, equipment, files, etc.

- *Seiso* – cleanliness. Everyone should help to keep things clean, organized, looking neat and attractive.

- *Seiketsu* – standardized clean-up. The regularity and institutionalization of keeping things clean and organized as part of 'visual management' is an effective means of continuous improvement.

- *Shitsuke* – discipline. Personal responsibility for living up to the other four S's can make or break the success of housekeeping.

Standardization of practices and institutionalization of the five S's will make it easier for everyone, including newcomers, throughout the organization to keep improving and building on the achieved success. Top management plays an important role in looking after the widespread implementation and co-ordination of kaizen, the five S's and the standardization of work.

The final analysis

The kaizen philosophy resonates well with speed of change at operational levels in the organization. The sustainability of improvements proposed and implemented by people on the work floor is perhaps the strongest argument in favour of kaizen. Its mere simplicity makes implementation easy, although some cultures may not be as receptive to the high level of self-discipline that the Japanese are able to keep up.

Kaizen has more potential in incremental change situations than in abrupt turnarounds. A culture that focuses on short-term success and big 'hits' is not the right ingredient for kaizen. Co-operation and widespread discipline at all levels of the organization are absolute keys to success.

Kay's distinctive capabilities

The big idea

In an efficient market, price always reflects the actual value of a product or service. Why, then, are some companies able to command higher prices for seemingly similar products? And why are some firms able to deliver more efficiently, or simply be the preferred supplier?

John Kay (1993) argues that successful creation and management of contracts and relationships within and around the enterprise create added value. In fact, Kay distinguishes three distinctive relational capabilities that allow companies to achieve competitive advantage: *architecture*, *reputation* and *innovation*. Additionally, a firm may have a competitive advantage through its command over strategic assets.

Kay's perspective

'Resource based theory sees the firm as a collection of assets, or capabilities. In the modern economy, most of these assets and capabilities are intangible. The success of corporations is based on those of their capabilities that are distinctive. Companies with distinctive capabilities have attributes which other cannot replicate, even once they have realized the benefit they offer to the company which originally possessed them.

Business strategy involves identifying a firm's capabilities: putting together a collection of complementary assets and capabilities, and maximizing and defending the economic rents which result. The concept of economic rent is central in linking the competitive advantage of the firm to conventional measures of performance.'

Architecture is a network of relational contracts within or around the organization, with employees (internal), and with suppliers and customers (external). Architecture can add value through organizational knowledge and routines, flexible response to change, and easy and open exchange of information.

These abilities allow for:

- creation and co-ordinated use of organizational knowledge;
- establishment of a co-operative ethic; and
- implementation of organizational routines.

Organizational knowledge, as defined by Kay, is more than the sum of the expertise of those who work in the firm, and is unavailable to other firms. Such knowledge could be specific to either a product, or a service, or a process.

It is important to understand that relational structures are a product of social and commercial values. These values develop throughout the history of an organization and cannot be easily created or changed. Distinctive capabilities related to architecture rest on relational contracting: there is a collective interest to co-ordinate efforts for the benefit of the organization.

Organizational routines increase efficiency and improve co-ordination. However, there is an inherent danger of the 'not invented here' syndrome.

Reputation is the most important commercial mechanism for conveying information to consumers in the initiation and maintenance of a business relationship.

When buyers search and experience goods, the seller wants to signal quality, so as to start a sequence of transactions in which to build up a relationship. But how does it start? Kay argues that buyer and seller enter into a sort of a Prisoner's Dilemma. Selling high quality for a high price is fair for both. Overselling (selling low quality for a high price) leads to a bad experience for the buyer, but a fantastic profit for the seller. Underselling ruins the seller's potential profit margin (efficient market), but is a great deal for the buyer. Selling low quality for a low price generally leaves both parties feeling like they've wasted their time. If either one of the players plays the game only once, then getting the one-time great deal is the best strategy. But otherwise, a fair deal is most beneficial for a long-term relationship.

Reputation helps assure the buyer of high quality when it cannot easily be determined. It is built up over time through:

- consumer's own experience;
- quality signals (e.g. price, promotion);
- demonstrations and free trials;
- self-imposed sanctions upon product failure, such as a warranty or guarantee;
- spreading reputation through word-of-mouth, promoting high ratings, brand leveraging etc.;

- association with other reputations and endorsements by influential people;
- staking the reputation once it is established.

A good reputation requires few resources to maintain, as long as the underlying quality is not compromised.

Innovation is the third primary distinctive capability. Innovation is often not successfully translated into competitive advantage. This failure is rooted in three issues:

1. costs and uncertainty of innovation process
2. innovation management
3. appropriate allocation of rewards.

The innovation process is costly and risky, because there is uncertainty about demand for a product, and whether there will be stiff competition. The innovating company faces a dilemma. There are two types of innovation games, both variants of the Prisoner's Dilemma: the Chicken Game and the Standards Game.

Chicken Game: if we assume that an innovation will be successful, the outcome of two competitors' possible decisions would be 'best' only when one decides to hold back. If the innovation fails, the firm that did not hold back will be ruined. The innovation game is very common in the pharmaceutical industry. The essence is that someone needs to swerve, as there is not enough room for all.

The *Standards Game* occurs in a market where products require complementary products (e.g. hardware and software). It doesn't matter which product becomes the standard, VHS or Betamax, everybody loses as long as there is no standard, and everybody wins when there is.

One possible strategy in these games is *commitment*: boldly announcing that the firm will not back off. This strategy, however, requires a reputation of doing so. Another strategy is simply being the first to market.

Finally, there is the issue of making sure that the innovation was worth the effort: is the innovation appropriable, for example, because of firm-specificity, or based on legal protection?

When to use it

There is no set methodology for using this model. Kay uses a lot of examples and game theory to illustrate the fundamental issues related to distinctive capabilities. The use of examples and training in game theory are key steps in narrowing the definition of true competitive advantage.

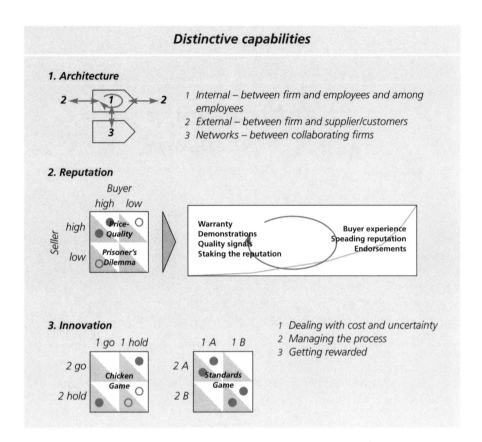

Distinctive capabilities

1. Architecture

2 ← 1 → 2

3

1 Internal – between firm and employees and among employees
2 External – between firm and supplier/customers
3 Networks – between collaborating firms

2. Reputation

Buyer
high   low

Seller

high   Price-Quality ○
low   Prisoner's Dilemma ○

Warranty
Demonstrations
Quality signals
Staking the reputation

Buyer experience
Speading reputation
Endorsements

3. Innovation

1 go 1 hold
2 go
2 hold   Chicken Game ○

1 A   1 B
2 A
2 B   Standards Game

1 Dealing with cost and uncertainty
2 Managing the process
3 Getting rewarded

The final analysis

Identification of distinctive capabilities with Kay's framework allows management to better understand the successes and failures in the history of the company. It may also help understand the values currently held as opposed to those that are desirable in order to increase competitiveness.

The main problem with Kay's framework is that it is as abstract as the distinctive capabilities it attempts to describe. As Kay puts it himself: if you can write it down, it can be copied.

Kotter's eight phases of change

The big idea

John Kotter (1990) studied over 100 companies going through change processes and decisively concluded that the following are the most common errors made (in this order):

1. *Allowing too much complacency.* It is a natural mistake to think that problems can be assessed and dealt with later.

2. *Failing to build a substantial coalition.* Countervailing forces, when not properly dealt with, will undermine the initiative sooner or later (most likely between cost incurred and objectives achieved).

3. *Underestimating the need for a clear vision.* Without a clear vision of the desired end result, a change effort can easily turn into a list of confusing, incompatible, and time-consuming projects going nowhere.

4. *Failing to clearly communicate the vision.* Even if management has a clear vision of the end result and the way to get there, it will not happen unless that vision is shared by all of those involved in its realization.

5. *Permitting roadblocks against the vision.* If organizational structures or old procedures remain intact despite their threat to the change effort, then this can be interpreted as poor commitment by subordinates.

6. *Not planning and getting short-term wins.* Without continuous reinforcement of the belief that the effort will be successful complex change efforts risk losing momentum. Employees may give up early, or worse, join the resistance.

1. Establish a sense of urgency	2. Create a coalition	3. Develop a clear vision	4. Share the vision	5. Empower people to clear obstacles	6. Secure short-term wins	7. Consolidate and keep moving	8. Anchor
■ Research market ■ Analyse competition ■ Identify and discuss (potential) crises and opportunities	■ For a powerful and influential group to lead the charge ■ Align this guiding coalition to work like a team	■ Create a vision to direct the change effort ■ Develop strategies to realize the vision	■ Use every possible way to communicate the new vision and strategies ■ Let guiding coalition members be role models for the rest of the organization	■ Get rid of obstacles ■ Change structures and systems that obstruct the change effort ■ Encourage risk taking and non-traditional ideas, activities and actions	■ Plan for visible performance improvements ■ 'Create' and declare the wins ■ Visibly recognize and reward those who made the wins possible	■ Build on gowing credibility to gradually change all systems, structures and policies that don't fit in the vision ■ Hire, promote and develop successful changers ■ Reinvigorate the change process with new projects, themes and change agents	■ Improve performance through customer and productivity orientation, and more effective leadership, and management

7. *Declaring victory too soon.* It is OK to celebrate a won battle, but the war may not be over. Until changes sink down deeply into the culture and systems, it is too early to declare victory.

8. *Not anchoring changes in corporate culture.* Change sticks only when it becomes 'the way we do things around here'.

When to use it

Kotter stresses the importance of using the sequence in the eight phases. After all, if the mission isn't clear, then how can you possibly communicate it successfully?

Different change efforts require different skill sets and attitudes. A crisis change process requires a leader, rather than a manager. Very large change efforts usually involve projects within projects, and projects with evolving visions. For example, an organization might be in a crisis when the change efforts start, but the end of the crisis is not necessarily the end of change. The result of multiple stages in the change effort can be complex, dynamic and very messy.

Kotter makes a clear distinction between management and leadership. Management is a set of processes that can keep a complex system of people and technology running smoothly. Leadership, on the other hand, defines the future, aligns people, and inspires them to pursue that vision. Kotter argues that too much emphasis is placed on *managing* change, whereas the key to success is in *leading* change.

The final analysis

Kotter notes that there are many more ways in which people manage to make mistakes in efforts of change. In fact, even successful change efforts are messy and full of surprises.

Anyone attempting to effectuate a change effort in an organizational setting should consider Kotter's model, if only for no other reason than to prevent making the 'usual mistakes', and be able to face challenges specific to the particular change effort in full capability.

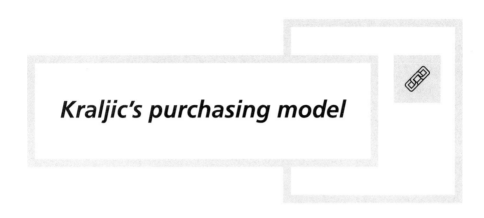

Kraljic's purchasing model

The big idea

Kraljic's (1983) purchasing model and the variations developed over the last decades help management select the most appropriate purchasing strategies for different types of products, thereby optimizing the trade-off between cost and risk. Costs include both the direct and indirect cost of purchasing, for example, management time, trouble shooting and drawing up contracts.

Two basic dimensions are included in Kraljic's matrix:

- impact on financial result
- supply risk (or uncertainty).

These two dimensions generate four quadrants, representing four categories of products:

- strategic products
- leverage products
- bottleneck products
- routine products.

When to use it

There are essentially three steps to making a Kraljic purchasing matrix for any company:

1. logical grouping of products
2. determining financial impact and risk
3. discerning purchasing categories in Kraljic's matrix (drawing the lines).

The first step, logical grouping of products is not as easy as it seems, and can be different per company. Typically, a full list of creditors makes a good starting point in determining a full list of products. A good rule of thumb in logically grouping the products is to argue whether or not the products are purchased or could reasonably be purchased from the same supplier(s), without considerably more or less effort. Nevertheless, logical grouping remains a critical and difficult first step.

Secondly, for each group of products formed in the first step, the impact on the financial result and the supply risk must be determined. Again, this is a fairly arbitrary process. Valuations on both dimensions are expressed relative to other valuations on the same dimensions. Most analysts will use indicators in the assessment of impact on financial result and in rating the supply risk.

The impact on the financial result is determined by such factors as:

- direct cost of the purchased product
- the percentage of total costs in the end product
- indirect cost of purchasing.

The supply risk can be determined by:

- number of suppliers
- availability of reserves or alternatives
- stability of (potential) supplier
- costs of switching to alternative supplier.

Common sense and management's knowledge of the market can result in any of the above risk factors being considered serious enough to decide upon labelling a particular (group of) products as 'high supply risk'.

The last step is to draw the lines that differentiate the four quadrants. Again, this is an arbitrary process. Often, an 80/20 line is drawn, but ultimately it depends on how focused management wants to be. A round figure or index can be chosen near the line; it makes sense not to break up the logical groups made in step 1, even in spite of the 80/20 line.

After the product groups have been differentiated using Kraljic's matrix, the following recommendations are generally believed to be proper actions to optimize the purchasing function.

Strategic products not only have a great impact on the bottom line, they are also hard to get or suppliers are difficult to replace. Partnerships and centralized buying is recommended. As these products carry a certain supply risk, it is important to establish long-term relationships or strategic partnerships. Suppliers of strategic products require serious management attention and effort from both companies to make the relationship work. Hence, the number of suppliers with which one can have such a strategic partnership is limited.

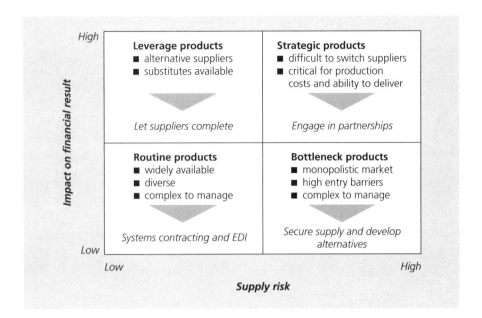

The **leverage products** group represents a large part of the impact that purchasing has on the company's financial result, but on the other hand there is an abundance of suppliers. Suppliers can thus be played out against each other. Tough as it may sound, the rules of the market dictate an equilibrium at a point where some suppliers may even go bankrupt as a result of the competitive squeeze – after all, the buyer can always choose another supplier. Leverage products require central contracts with general terms and conditions. Many companies choose to have multiple suppliers in order to play them out against each other.

Strategic and leverage products usually make up 80 per cent of total purchasing, yet require no more than 20 per cent of the effort. Extra attention to these products can yield great savings though, for example through volume discounts. It is also possible to work on product quality improvements, delivery reliability, product development and cost reduction.

Less 'strategic', but interesting nevertheless, are the so-called **bottleneck products**. Disruption of supply would have serious consequences for the company. The company must secure supply or be protected against lack of it. This usually leads to extra inventory, hedging and/or supplier contracts with major penalties for breach or break of contract.

Routine products are typically office supplies, catering etc. Although there is potential for savings, purchasing management should not focus on these products. The company can have a limited number of suppliers for a whole range of products, allowing for streamlined administrative handling and discount negotiations.

The final analysis

Kraljic's purchasing model helps companies to avoid being 'penny wise and pound foolish' in purchasing management. It is relatively easy to implement and, once accepted, can have a major impact on the financial result. Not every company has purchasing management at the top of its agenda, though.

In a quest for top-line growth, many organizations pay more attention to marketing and sales management than to purchasing management. However, purchasing management not only has a significant impact on the bottom line, it increasingly determines the value delivered to customers as they become more knowledgeable of products and processes. Furthermore, increasing numbers of companies are deciding to buy or outsource (parts) of products or processes, making purchasing management even more important.

The decisive and prescriptive nature of Kraljic's model can have a profound impact on how a company manages its purchasing process. However, emotional and relational aspects may mar the outcome, especially when insufficient room is given to translate such aspects in the analyses. At the end of the day, management will make its own decisions, supported by the differentiation made using the model.

A glass manufacturer reorganized its purchasing management in the wake of a company-wide business redesign. In the first phase, the Kraljic purchasing model proved to be of great help in developing an overview of the purchasing segments, i.e. groups of products requiring similar management attention and treatment. By plotting the segments in Kraljic's matrix it was possible to identify the segments with the greatest impact on financial results, as well as those with the highest supply risk.

Together, Berenschot consultants and purchasing managers subsequently devised a purchasing strategy for each segment, using the Kraljic model as a general guide, combined with everyday hands-on experience. Special attention was paid to the 'leverage' segments and the 'strategic' segments, resulting in significant savings in 'leverage' products and improved co-ordination of logistical processes with suppliers.

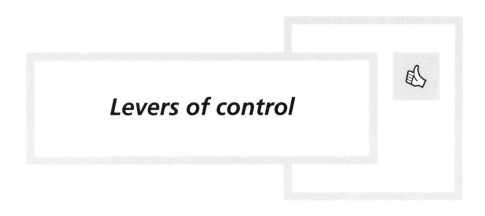

Levers of control

The big idea

Monitoring and measuring the achievement of pre-set goals is relatively easy in small organizations. But as organizations grow larger and more complex, and competitive environments become more dynamic, traditional strict methods of control no longer work. In fact, control processes tend to clash with creativity, initiative and risk-taking.

Robert Simons (1995) proposes a framework with four levers of control that managers in medium and large-sized organizations can use to manage the tension between creation and control. The core purpose of the framework is to analyse and act upon the control of the company's business strategy. The four levers of control relate to the four constructs for successful strategy implementation: core values, risks to be avoided, strategic uncertainties and critical performance variables.

The four levers create opposing forces. When used correctly, these levers allow senior management in large companies to develop and reflect core values, reveal opinions and insight from subordinates, increase the probability of goal achievement and increase the organization's chances of survival and prosperity.

When to use it

In order to use the levers properly, senior management must start by *understanding* the levers and the constructs they work on. For each lever, management must define ambitions, measure the status quo and track changes.

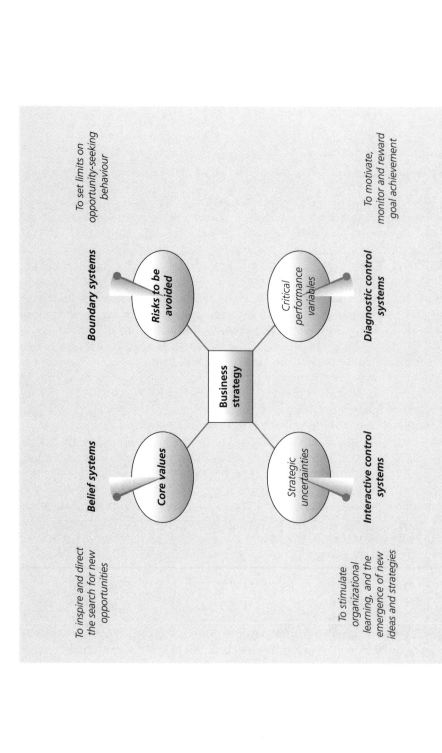

To set limits on opportunity-seeking behaviour

To motivate, monitor and reward goal achievement

Boundary systems

Risks to be avoided

Diagnostic control systems

Critical performance variables

Business strategy

Belief systems

Core Values

Interactive control systems

Strategic uncertainties

To inspire and direct the search for new opportunities

To stimulate organizational learning, and the emergence of new ideas and strategies

Belief systems are sets of explicit beliefs that define basic values, purpose, and direction on:

- how value is created
- the level of performance desired
- human relationships.

Boundary systems are formally stated rules, limits and proscriptions tied to defined sanctions and credible threats of punishment.

Diagnostic control systems are feedback systems that monitor organizational outcomes and prompt to correct deviations from pre-set standards of performance, such as targets, budgets, output standards, etc.

Interactive control systems require regular direct personal involvement of managers in the decision-making activities of their subordinates, for example, in project management, market analyses, budgeting, etc.

The next step for management is to know *how* and *when* to use the levers.

Belief systems are communicated through mission statements, vision statements, credos and statements of purpose. These are tricky and only applicable when:

- opportunities grow rapidly
- top management overhauls strategy
- top management wants to create momentum.

Boundary systems are put in place through codes of conduct, predefined strategic planning methods, asset acquisition regulations, and operational guidelines. Business conduct boundaries are particularly important when the cost of maintaining an organization's reputation is high (i.e. to protect the good name and/or brand). Strategic boundaries are most important when the resources for new initiatives and/or business development are limited, i.e. when the firm needs to stay focused.

Diagnostic control systems require that management sets standards, measures outputs and links incentives to goal achievement. Standards can be set when, for instance, (re)designing a process, (re)assigning responsibilities, or (re)distributing tasks. Output measurement should take place when output is available, and when it can be used to influence or correct a process that is malfunctioning. Whenever the output or the process is of critical importance and capable of being linked to performance, incentives should be offered.

Interactive control systems are most effective when process data (input and output) are incorporated into management interaction. Management should always pay sufficient attention to the primary process and participate in face-to-face meetings with subordinates. By challenging data, assumptions and action plans, management can stimulate active pursuit of high performance by subordinates.

The final analysis

Simons has done an admirable job in organizing a large number of ideas on organizational control. Most notably, this framework shows how management control can be used to facilitate change and organizational development, rather than as a method of constraining wild corporate growth.

This book can bring the CEO and the CFO together. There is, however, also a down side to introducing management control to general management: whenever a model requires top-management involvement in frameworks and control procedures, it runs the risk of becoming too much of an academic exercise, or simply said: too much work.

MABA analysis

The big idea

A MABA analysis compares the relative *market attractiveness* (MA) of a business activity or product-market combination with the *business attractiveness* (BA), as determined by the ability to operate in a product-market combination. The MABA analysis is therefore a useful tool when making decisions related to the business portfolio.

Market attractiveness is determined by external indicators such as:

- profit margins
- size of the market
- market growth (expectations)
- concentration
- stability
- competitiveness.

Porter's five forces analysis and the BCG matrix could be used as determinants for these indicators.

When to use it

Business attractiveness is largely determined by company-related indicators, such as the extent to which the product-market combination, market segment or business activity is a logical match with your company's current products, services, activities or competencies. Your own organization's position in the value chain or network of suppliers and customers is also of relevance: can you benefit from economies of scale or other synergetic effects by taking on a particular product-market combination?

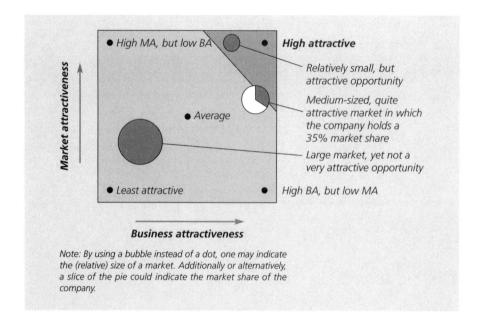

Note: By using a bubble instead of a dot, one may indicate the (relative) size of a market. Additionally or alternatively, a slice of the pie could indicate the market share of the company.

The first step in making a MABA analysis is to decide which indicators you deem important in determining the two dimensions of attractiveness and how important they are (weighting). It goes without saying that an independently derived set of indicators and weights will lead to more objective results. If possible, quantification of indicators helps in creating a scale.

Step two is to define the product-market combinations, the opportunities, the segments or the activities that will be subject to the MABA analysis. Although these need not be mutually exclusive, one important factor to take into account is the extent to which one opportunity affects the attractiveness of another.

The MABA analysis is most often used for analysis and presentation of new opportunities. Corporate and business development managers, as well as consultants, find it very useful to put the most attractive opportunities in either the top-left or the top-right corner. Some analysts create quadrants or more blocks Another way of emphasizing the most attractive opportunities or weeding out the better from the worse is the application of curved or diagonal lines that serve as separators or thresholds.

There are many variations on the MABA analysis. The most common addition is the use of 'bubbles' to indicate one or even two extra dimensions, usually market size in units or currency, with a pie slice to indicate market share.

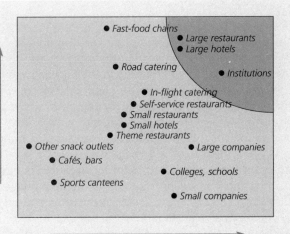

Market attractiveness
- Product match
- Current position in channel
- Buyers' concentration
- Homogeneity

- Fast-food chains
- Large restaurants
- Large hotels
- Road catering
- Institutions
- In-flight catering
- Self-service restaurants
- Small restaurants
- Small hotels
- Theme restaurants
- Other snack outlets
- Large companies
- Cafés, bars
- Colleges, schools
- Sports canteens
- Small companies

Business attractiveness
- Growth
- Size
- Profitability/margins
- Outlet concentration
- Competition

A major food-producing company wanted to enter the second stage of development of its professional foods division. With so many new opportunities and a relatively immature organization for this market, a MABA analysis was conducted.

The actual MABA analysis was carried out in a number of stages. We performed three major partial MABA analyses:

- average annual growth % v. relative activity in the PMC (product-market-channel) combination with bubbles indicating market size;

- individual product level analysis of penetration of products in channels v. the product's relative importance in the channels based on average per outlet turnover product relative to all products;

- the company's relative growth in all of the relevant market v. the average annual growth of these markets (comparable with BCG's growth-share matrix) with pie sliced bubbles.

The MABA analysis helped our client to identify three major opportunities, while the process of identifying of product-market combinations in itself led to a new organizational structure.

Note: As in most cases, reality proved far more complex than can be captured in a single MABA analysis. The underlying analyses for assessing the market and business attractiveness were more extensive than can be described in this context.

The final analysis

The MABA analysis is a very powerful model to help companies prioritize new opportunities. Especially in situations of scarcity of funds or management time, the model proves of great service in making decisions. However, MABA is much less powerful when discussing existing businesses. Those involved usually have a very strong ability and willingness to challenge assumptions and indicator ratings to such a level of detail that the model loses its most profound quality: to simplify a complex situation.

The Achilles' heel of the MABA analysis is in choosing and weighting indicators; different indicators and weights can lead to very different results. There is also a danger of creating a false sense of objectivity when the indicators are quantified: quantification only improves accuracy on the subjectively chosen scale.

The MABA analysis is limited to two (or three) artificially combined dimensions. Many more extensive MABA analyses are performed using different indicators to compensate for this weakness.

The Malcolm Baldridge Award

The big idea

Established by the US Congress in 1987 and named after former Secretary of Commerce, Malcolm Baldrige, this award aims to promote quality awareness.

The award is based on a weighted score of seven categories of performance criteria:

- leadership
- strategic planning
- customer and market focus
- information and analysis
- human resource development and management
- process management
- business results.

The criteria are based on a set of core values and concepts that are embedded in well-managed and successful organizations. The maximum attainable score is 1000 points, divided over 18 sub-criteria of the seven categories. Modifications to the weights and specific aspects of each of the criteria are made regularly by the National Institute of Standards and Technology (NIST). We refer to the NIST website (below) for a more detailed description of the categories of performance criteria.

The **leadership** category refers to how leadership is exercised, how it is structured and developed, and how decisions are made. High scores in this category require effective leadership based on clear values, challenging, yet attainable expectations, support and rewards for initiative, a widespread sense of purpose and short chains of command. When it comes to how the organization is viewed by the public, leaders are expected to hold a governing role: corporate communication, environmental

Categories/Items		Point values
Leadership		**120**
1.1	Organizational leadership	80
1.2	Public responsibility and citizenship	40
Strategic planning		**85**
2.1	Strategy development	40
2.2	Strategy deployment	45
Customer and market focus		**85**
3.1	Customer and market knowledge	40
3.2	Customer relationships and satisfaction	45
Information and analysis		**90**
4.1	Measurement and analysis of organizational performance	50
4.2	Information management	40
Human resource focus		**85**
5.1	Work systems	35
5.2	Employee education, training and development	25
5.3	Employee well-being and satisfaction	25
Process management		**85**
6.1	Product and service processes	45
6.2	Business processes	25
6.3	Support processes	15
Business results		**450**
7.1	Customer-focused results	125
7.2	Financial and market results	125
7.3	Human resources results	80
7.4	Organizational effectiveness results	120
TOTAL POINTS		**1000**

awareness and respect for the local economy are key elements in the corporation's 'citizenship'.

In the second category, the process of **strategic planning**, how plans are employed throughout the organization and plan performance tracking are subject to scrutiny. Key scoring factors are organizational alignment related to strategic planning and the extent to which strategic plans reflect the company's focus on the future.

How a company determines its **focus on customer and market** requirements, preferences, satisfaction, and how it builds customer relationships comprises the third performance category. High scores are awarded to those companies that have systematic approaches to gather customer and market intelligence. As customer loyalty is a key to future revenues, successful efforts in the discipline of retaining and developing customers are an important scoring criterion.

The **performance measurement** category considers how the organization measures performance, as well as how measurement data is analysed and reviewed. The underlying core Baldrige value is 'management by fact'.

The **HRM** category examines how employees can develop and utilize their full potential. Does the company maintain culture that stimulates performance excellence and personal improvement? Are training and development offered to further individual development?

The more systematically a company goes about its **process management**, the better the assessment in this category. At the same time, this should not get in the way of flexibility. Continuous improvement should be driven by the relentless pursuit of problem prevention.

Finally, the **business results** should speak for themselves after all the efforts described in the first six categories. Expect relative performance level assessment, based on competitive and industry benchmarks.

When to use it

Companies can use the Baldrige criteria to assess their management systems and identify the most vital areas for improvement. Common reasons identified by companies to assess their management systems with these criteria are market changes, the desire to remain competitive, instigating or enhancing organizational learning, jump-starting change initiatives by improving awareness of the company's state of affairs, and focusing the organization on common goals.

The NIST issues brochures and maintains a website **(www.quality.nist.gov)** to help companies to use the Baldrige framework, the criteria and a 10-step approach to self-assessment, the latter is presented on p. 130.

Self-assessment requires support throughout the organization. Indicators of readiness for self-assessment are:

- senior leaders are aware of key issues, but need 'buy-in' to take action;
- senior leaders support self-assessment and consecutive actions;
- positive reactions from opinion leaders;
- champions for self-assessment are available.

1. Boundary setting	2. Champions	3. Format and scope	4. Organizational profile	5. Practice	6. Teamwork	7. Strengths and gaps	8. Focus	9. Action plan	10. Evaluation
Identify the boundaries of the organization to be assessed. Clarify what parts of the organization are included, if not all, and indicate what will be evaluated.	Select **seven champions**, one for each of the criteria. These people must have leadership and facilitation skills, as well as widespread knowledge of the organization.	Decide on the format and scope of the assessment, including **data gathering, communication and action plans**.	Senior leaders and champions make the organizational profile.	Category champions **learn how to use the** criteria for self-assessment by practising likely responses to the questions and gap analyses and comparing them with **response guidelines**.	Champions each select 3–5 **category team members**.	**Share responses** among teams and finalize findings.	Identify the organization's **key strengths** and prioritize **opportunities** for improvement.	Champions develop and oversee the implementation of an action plan for improvement.	Champions receive **feedback** and evaluate the process of self-assessment, as well as the action plan.
■ To ensure that all appropriate areas are included	■ To participate in preparing the organizational profile and responses to category item questions	■ To allow all participants to provide perspectives about the organization in an agreed upon format	■ **Organizational environment:** products, services, mission, vision, values, culture, employee profiles, major technologies, regulatory context, financial structure	■ To learn how to use the criteria for self-assessment and action	Using the team members' expertise and ability to provide relevant data and information, detailed responses are formulated to the criteria questions.	**Identify key strengths and gaps** in category responses.	■ To be able to develop an action plan that most effectively uses the available resources	Include **short-term actions to maintain momentum** for change in the organization.	Pursue feedback and schedule regular evaluation sessions and perform a schedule **reassessment** to measure the rate of improvement.
■ To ensure data will be consistent			■ **Organizational relationships:** key customers, markets, suppliers, dealers, requirements		External members may be useful to provide independent perspectives from external relationships.	Leverage the broad perspective of multiple teams to identify **overall themes** that cut across categories.		The plan should include specific tasks, key progress dates, methods of result measurement and accountability.	
■ To ensure appropriate staffing on each of the criteria			■ **Competitive position**		The business results category team interacts with all other teams to link results to approaches.	■ To get a common understanding of what and how the organization is doing		Senior leaders must **communicate** the plan to the organization, and **reward** the organization and its achieving members for progress.	
			■ **Strategic challenge**						
			■ **Performance management**						

The final analysis

The Malcolm Baldrige Award has great value for organizations willing to embark on a path of continuous improvement. NIST has compared award winners to the S&P 500 and concluded that Baldrige Award winners have consistently outperformed the S&P 500 by 4.4 to 1.

Of course, the Baldrige Award on its own cannot guarantee great business results: additional ingredients for success such as entrepreneurship, innovation and a healthy business climate are also required.

The marketing mix

The big idea

While the marketing concept refers to an organization's goal of trying to satisfy customers' needs by means of a co-ordinated set of activities, marketing strategy is the method an organization selects to achieve this goal, namely the selection and analysis of a target market. Having identified suitable target markets for its products, you must subsequently create and maintain an appropriate *marketing mix*.

Commonly known as the 'Four Ps' (*product*, *place*, *promotion*, *price*), the marketing mix is a tactical toolkit that an organization can put to use to realize its strategy. The marketing mix thus forms an integral part of marketing strategy. The four components comprising the toolkit are largely controllable by the organization. They, therefore, can be adjusted on an ongoing basis to keep pace with the changing needs of the target group in question, as well as the various forces within the marketing environment.

The function of the marketing mix is to help develop a package that will not only satisfy the needs of the customers within the target markets, but simultaneously maximize your organization's performance.

When to use it

There are three basic steps:

1. Research – to develop a marketing mix that precisely matches the needs of the customers in your target market you first have to gather information.

2. Analyse the variables in turn – determine the optimum mix, i.e. the one that will allow you to strike a balance between satisfying your customers and maximizing your own organization's profitability.

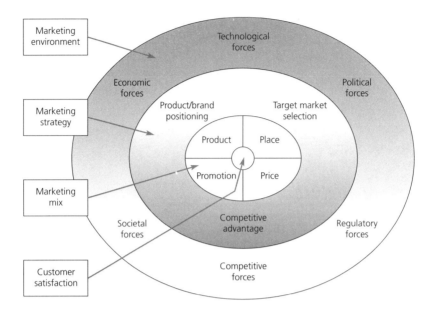

- *Product*. Do you actually produce what your customers want? Possible decisions and activities include new product development, modification of existing products, and elimination of products that are no longer attractive or that are unprofitable. There is also a variety of activities closely linked to the product that can be considered, such as branding, packaging, guarantees and the handling of complaints.

- *Place* (distribution). Are your products available in the right quantities, in the right place, at the right time? And can you achieve this whilst keeping inventory, transport and storage costs as low as possible? Analyse and compare the various distribution possibilities, after which the most appropriate option can be selected. Again, there is a number of activities related to the place variable, such as selecting and motivating intermediaries, controlling inventory and managing transport and storage as efficiently as possible.

- *Promotion*. How can you best inform/educate groups of customers about your organization and its products? Different types of promotional activities may be necessary depending on whether the organization wishes to launch a new product, to increase awareness with regard to special features of an existing one, or to retain interest in a product that has been available in the same form for a long time. Decisions must therefore be taken as to the most effective way of delivering the desired message to the target group.

- *Price*. How much are your customers willing to pay? The value obtained in an exchange is critical to consumers, in addition to which price is often used as a competitive tool, not only in price wars but also for image enhancement. Pricing decisions are thus highly sensitive.

3. Check – monitoring and control on an ongoing basis are essential to ascertain the effectiveness of the chosen mix and also how well it is being executed.

The final analysis

One of the problems with the 'Four Ps' is that they have a tendency to keep increasing in number, prompting the question 'Where does marketing stop?'. Of all the candidates, the 'people' factor is undoubtedly the most widely accepted fifth 'P'. After all, people manipulate the marketing mix as marketers; they make products/services available to marketplace as intermediaries; they create the need for marketing as consumers/ buyers; they play an important role when it comes to service levels, recruitment, training, retention, etc.

It is tempting to view the marketing mix variables as controllable, but remember that there are limits – price changes may be restricted by economic conditions or government regulations; changes in design and promotion are expensive and cannot be effected overnight; people are expensive to hire and train, etc. Do not forget to keep an eye on what is happening in the outside world, as some events may have a greater impact than you think.

At the end of the day, successful marketing has a lot to do with gut feeling and acting on hunches. While the marketing mix is a useful aid when it comes to analysing and ordering the multitude of things to be considered, it is, and remains, a tool. In other words, if you really believe in something, go for it – have the courage of your own convictions! There are plenty of success stories (Honda in the USA) to prove that gambling can pay off.

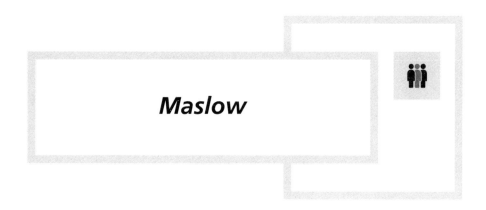

Maslow

The big idea

An eminent psychologist, Maslow was fascinated by the question of what motivates people. His observations led him to conclude that, as a species, human beings constantly strive to fulfil a variety of needs. Basic needs, such as food, warmth and shelter come first (physical needs), followed by more complex emotional needs in the middle (social needs). Finally, there are more abstract needs, such as 'self-actualization' (personal needs):

1. physiological needs
2. certainty
3. social acceptance
4. appreciation
5. self-actualization.

No sooner are the desires at one level met, people turn their attention to those at the next level. It, therefore, follows that our priorities change along with developments in the standard of living: in developed countries, food is now much more than simply fuel, and work is much more than just a way of earning money to survive. However, not all individuals ultimately reach the top of the pyramid, hence the form chosen: the higher the level, the fewer people will attain it.

When to use it

Traditionally viewed as a tool to help understand consumer motivation, Maslow's pyramid is referred to in many marketing works. Recently, however, the growing difficulty and expense involved in recruiting and

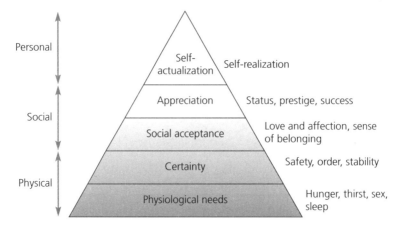

subsequently retaining the 'right' employees, has prompted closer investigation of just what it is that attracts and motivates people. Maslow's pyramid has consequently come to be seen as an important aid in gaining a better understanding of the psychological forces affecting employee motivation.

Attracting and retaining employees involves being able to present them with attractive working conditions and/or remuneration packages.

Ten Have *et al*. (2000) have defined two important concepts that can be helpful in this respect:

- the binding portfolio – all the elements within a company that can help to bind and motivate employees;
- the motivation mix – the specific combination of elements that characterize a certain type of employee.

Employees come in all shapes and sizes. Even though each individual has his or her own extensive list of needs and demands, they can be roughly divided into types depending on the similarities in their needs. By grouping these needs and creating a binding portfolio that meets them, binding can be encouraged, furthermore in an efficient way.

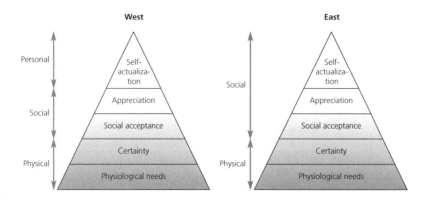

The final analysis

Despite globalization, huge cultural differences still exist throughout the world. One needs to bear in mind that Maslow's needs hierarchy is based very much on American/western European norms and values, and takes no account of these cultural differences. In Asia, for instance, the 'social' needs are much more important than personal.

The needs hierarchy is and remains a valuable tool for understanding what motivates people, however, particularly when used in combination with Hofstede's cultural dimensions.

The 7-S framework

The big idea

The McKinsey 7-S framework was originally developed as a way of thinking more broadly about effectively organizing a company. Rather than thinking in terms of strategy implementation as a matter of strategy and structure, one must think comprehensively about a strategy and how it works in conjunction with a variety of other elements. The seven Ss are:

- shared values
- strategy
- structure
- systems
- skills
- staff
- style.

The seven organizational elements or dimensions can be divided into what are called 'hard' and 'soft' elements. The underlying thought is to stress the importance of the so-called 'soft' elements in reaction to their negligence.

'Hard' (or tangible) elements are strategy, structure and systems:

Strategy refers to the organization's objectives and the conscious choices it makes in order to achieve them, such as prioritizing certain products and markets, and allocating resources.

Structure refers to the organizational structure, hierarchy and co-ordination, including division and integration of tasks and activities.

Systems are the primary and secondary processes that the organization employs to get things done, such as manufacturing systems, supply planning, order taking processes, etc.

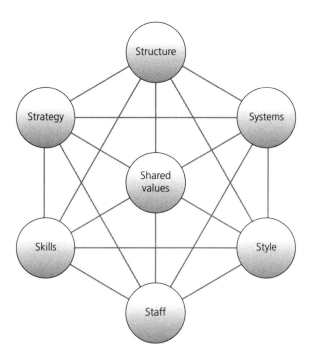

'Soft' elements are shared values, style, staff and skills:

Shared values are those that underlie the very reason for existence of the company. They include the core beliefs and expectations that people have of their company.

Style refers to the unwritten yet tangible evidence of how management really sets priorities and spends its time. Symbolic behaviour and the way bosses relate to their workers are the indicators of the organization's style.

The **staff** is comprised of the people in an organization and, in particular, their collective presence.

Skills are organizational capabilities that are *independent* of individuals, a concept that is often misunderstood. Pascale (1996), who was involved in developing the 7-S framework, argues that skills are both 'soft' and 'hard'. He sees them as the distinctive capabilities that truly set a company apart (compare with Kay's Distinctive Capabilities). Skills are dependent upon the six other Ss.

When to use it

Although Waterman, Peters and Philips intended that their brainchild be used in a much more sophisticated way, the 7-S framework is nonetheless a good checklist to define and analyse the most important elements or dimensions of an organization. The framework imposes discipline on the researcher, allowing for both 'soft' and 'hard' perspectives.

The 7-S framework can be used as a means of assessing the viability of a strategic plan from the perspective of the organization's ability to succeed at the proposed strategy. In this case, says Waterman, think of the 7-Ss as compasses and consider whether or not they are all pointing in the same direction. For example, make sure that you're not proposing to opt for a strategic direction that rubs against the shared values in the company or that requires skills that the organization simply does not have.

In addition to the 'atomic' illustration, the framework needs a matrix or table of some kind that helps the analyst structure the assessment of the proposed strategy against the 7-Ss of an organization.

Construct a matrix in which conflicts and possible solutions on combinations of S are listed. Then make a decision on how to either adjust the strategy or make changes to the organization to enable the strategy (in the

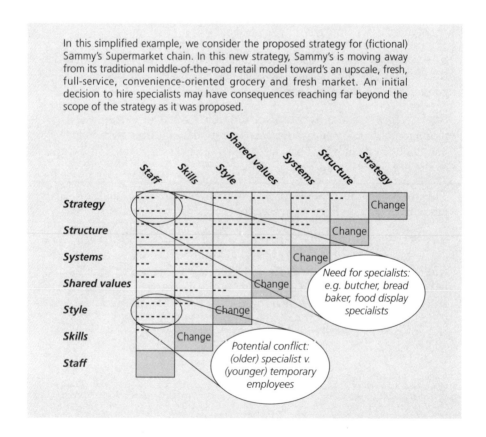

In this simplified example, we consider the proposed strategy for (fictional) Sammy's Supermarket chain. In this new strategy, Sammy's is moving away from its traditional middle-of-the-road retail model toward's an upscale, fresh, full-service, convenience-oriented grocery and fresh market. An initial decision to hire specialists may have consequences reaching far beyond the scope of the strategy as it was proposed.

near future). When used like this with discipline, the 7-S framework can help make a strategy more 'wholesome' than most strategies have ever been.

Pascale argues that a firm's success depends on the successful management of vectors of contention (opposing poles) on the 7-S dimensions. The smartest companies use conflict to their advantage. Although seemingly paradoxical, they power the engine of inquiry in pursuit of excellence. To illustrate this point, consider the example for strategy: although it is important to analyse strategic options, big breakthroughs usually come from opportunistic home runs, such as Honda's entry into the US motorcycle market. Howard Head, on the other hand, failed to bring it home with his invention of the metal ski – other entrepreneurs beat him to it. By analysing and understanding the wider implications of his innovation, they were able to jump on the redefinition of the sports equipment market.

The seven Ss as vectors of contention

Strategy	Planned	←——→	Opportunistic
Structure	Elitist	←——→	Pluralist
Systems	Mandatory	←——→	Discretionary
Shared values	Hard minds	←——→	Soft hearts
Style	Managerial	←——→	Transformational
Staff	Collegiality	←——→	Individuality
Skills	Maximize	←——→	'Meta-mize'

The final analysis

The very essence of the McKinsey 7-S model is simultaneously the greatest hurdle for its use: to make the 'soft' elements specific.

Consequently, the 7-S framework is often used in a dressed-down manner: to list issues along a checklist. The integral use of the framework, either by analysing the relations between the Ss, or by analysing organizational conflicts within Ss, is often omitted. On the other hand, many more models can be applied on the level of the individual Ss, unlocking a potential perhaps unforeseen even by the authors of the 7-S framework.

Mintzberg's configurations

The big idea

Using Henry Mintzberg's basic organizational configurations, one can categorize or even typify organizations. This serves mainly as a means of understanding what drives decisions and activities.

Mintzberg explains that there are:

- six basic parts of an organization
- six co-ordinating mechanisms
- six types of decentralization.

The essence is to assume that a limited number of configurations can help explain much of what is observed in organizations. In fact, there is a fundamental correspondence between all of the 'sixes'. The result is that there can be six plus one organizational configurations, the last being the result of lack of a real co-ordinating mechanism:

1. entrepreneurial organization

2. machine organization

3. professional organization

4. diversified organization

5. innovative organization

6. missionary organization

   + 1 political organization.

The basic configurations help to discern organizations and their (typical) core problems. Using the basic configurations can help to prevent 'wrong' organizational structures and ineffective co-ordination of activities.

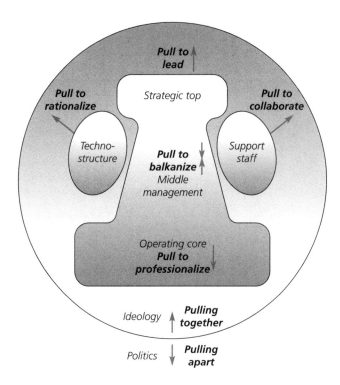

When to use it

In order to use Mintzberg's (1990) configurations to analyse and redesign (parts of) an organization, one should start with the identification of its basic parts. Each organization, Mintzberg says in his revised writing on the structuring of organizations, consists of a maximum of six basic parts:

1. operating core
2. strategic top
3. middle management
4. technostructure
5. support staff
6. ideology.

The first three are typically connected through a single chain of formal authority and thus depicted as one piece. The technostructure and support staff on either side influence the core indirectly, while the ideology represents the norms and values (the 'strong culture') that surround, yet penetrate the very fabric of the organization. These six organizational building blocks are internal influencers of the direction of an organization. In addition, there are various outside forces, such as shareholders, suppliers and customers, all of which have an impact on the organization.

Configuration	Prime co-ordinating mechanism	Key part of organization	Type of decentralization
Entrepreneurial organization	Direct supervision	Strategic top	Vertical and horizontal centralization
Machine organization	Standardization of work	Technostructure	Limited horizontal decentralization
Professional organization	Standardization of skills	Operating core	Horizontal decentralization
Diversified organization	Standardization of output	Middle management	Limited vertical decentralization
Innovative organization	Mutual adjustment	Support staff	Selected decentralization
Missionary organization	Standardization of norms	Ideology	Decentralization
Political organization	None	None	Any

After correctly identifying the organizational parts, determine and/or analyse alternative co-ordinating mechanisms. As labour and influence are divided among the parts of the organization, there are several co-ordinating mechanisms that determine the structure of an organization. When organizations lack a co-ordination mechanism, they are more likely to become politicized as a result of parts fighting to fill the power vacuum. Mintzberg distinguishes six co-ordinating mechanisms:

1. mutual adjustment (by co-workers in the operational core co-ordinate each other);

2. direct supervision;

3. standardization of work (through procedures, systems, etc.);

4. standardization of outputs (through specifications, targets, etc.);

5. standardization of skills (through education and expectations of a worker's ability to fulfil a task);

6. standardization of norms (through a common set of beliefs of how things are done or achieved).

Which co-ordinating mechanism is the most predominant? Is that how it should be? Suppose changes are needed – what can you do? The essence of organizational design is the manipulation of design parameters, says Mintzberg. Parameters of structural design are:

- job specialization
- behaviour specialization
- training
- indoctrination
- unit grouping
- unit size
- planning and control systems
- liaison devices (positions, task forces, committees, integration managers, matrix structure, etc.).

However, most important parameter in Mintzberg's model is the way in which power is divided throughout the organization:

- decentralization (six types):

  1. vertical and horizontal centralization (strategic top rules);

  2. limited horizontal decentralization (strategic top shares power with technostructure that standardizes work for all);

  3. limited vertical decentralization (power delegated to middle management or BU level);

  4. vertical and horizontal decentralization (power mainly at the operating core);

  5. selective horizontal and vertical decentralization (power dispersed at various levels);

  6. pure decentralization (power shared equally throughout).

Additionally, several situational factors mostly beyond your control influence the choice of the design parameters:

- age and size of the organization
- technical system
- the (competitive) environment
- external power and control.

Not only can you determine into which category your organization falls, you can also determine what changes are needed to make it internally consistent.

For example, in a **professional organization**, or rather, in an organization of professionals, the operational core is a strong block. The strategic top needs and gets continuous flow of information by strong vertical and horizontal decentralization. The professionals in the operational core, clients' loyalty and know-how are the organization's main 'assets'. Operational skills are standardized. Consulting firms and law firms are good examples.

Alternatively, in a typical **entrepreneurial organization**, the strategic top is the most dominant. Direct supervision is the primary co-ordination mechanism. The organization is very centralized.

The final analysis

The robust nature of the configurations introduces the danger of using them as blueprints. The relatively limited number of criteria to define the organizational configurations makes it difficult for organizations to 'fit' or even compare to the typical configurations. To speak to this point, Mintzberg argues that many organizations are hybrids or mixtures of multiple configurations.

In our opinion, it doesn't matter whether or not an organization can be exactly classified as innovative or entrepreneurial. More important is that Mintzberg's model helps to understand the relationship between the nature of an organization and its co-ordination mechanisms. As Mintzberg says, there is no one right way to manage an organization: what's good for General Motors is often completely wrong for Joe's Body Shop.

Mintzberg's management roles

The big idea

At the beginning of the 20th century, the French industrialist Henri Fayol described the task of managers as being a combination of organization, co-ordination, planning and control. Despite dominating management vocabulary for around three-quarters of a century, Henry Mintzberg was not convinced that these four activities cover what managers actually do. He, therefore, carried out extensive research within a number of organizations, in the process disproving a number of myths.

Myth 1:
Managers are reflective, systematic planners.
Fact:
Managers work at an unrelenting pace; their activities are characterized by brevity, variety and discontinuity; they are strongly oriented to action and dislike reflective activities.

Myth 2:
Effective managers have no regular duties to perform.
Fact:
Managers perform a number of regular duties, including ritual and ceremony, negotiations, and processing soft information linking the organization to its environment.

Myth 3:
Senior managers need aggregated information, best provided by a formal management information system.
Fact:
Managers prefer verbal media, telephone calls and meetings to documents.

Myth 4:
Management is a science and a profession.
Fact:
Managers' programmes (scheduling time, processing information, decision-making, etc.) are locked inside their brains.

As a result of his research, Mintzberg came up with a basic description of managerial work. Using formal authority and status as a starting point, he identified 10 roles of managers: three interpersonal roles, which in turn give rise to three informational ones, followed by four decisional ones. Together, these 10 roles form an integrated whole, no one part of which can remain intact having been separated from the rest.

Based closely on the facts uncovered by his research, Mintzberg subsequently drew up a series of self-study questions for managers. By considering these questions in the light of the 'facts' as opposed to the 'myths' regarding the way in which they tend to work, managers are encouraged to find ways to circumvent potential problems.

Take for instance, the danger of placing what amounts to the databank in the heads of the managers – what happens when they are unavailable, or if they leave the company? Here the challenge is to develop an efficient system for sharing privileged information. And if a manager's way of working is characterized by brevity, variety and discontinuity, how can all the bits and pieces ever be knitted together to form an integrated whole?

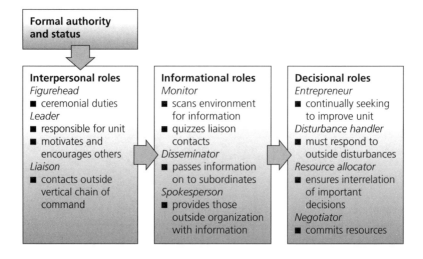

When to use it

The main value of the models lies in the fact that they provide managers with a frame of reference. Consider your own work: which roles do you fulfil? Go through the roles in turn and for each one give yourself a score out of 10. Low scores indicate weak areas, i.e. those to which more attention must be paid.

The final analysis

Mintzberg's roles are not intended to be prescriptive. Instead, they serve as a looking glass, providing managers with an insight into how they spend their time. Just drawing attention to the problems can go a long way towards remedying them.

By dispelling the myths and highlighting the real nature of their work, managers can focus on how they can avoid the pitfalls and work in a more effective manner.

Despite the exponential growth in the number of management schools, according to Mintzberg, most focus on imparting knowledge on specialist areas such as accounting or marketing, rather than the skills needed to manage: resolving conflicts, establishing information networks, disseminating information, etc. At present, therefore, it is only by being introspective that managers can successfully learn 'on the job'.

The neurotic organization

The big idea

Five forms of organizational neurosis have been identified by Kets de Vries and Miller (1984):

- paranoid
- compulsive
- dramatic
- depressive
- schizoid.

Each of these dysfunctions is rooted in a combination of individual and collective experiences. Often this leads to a distorted or limited perspective of the environment, or even within the organization. Leaders, or those who are supposed to fulfil the role, are frequently personally affected: they have a fantasy that reinforces their dysfunctional behaviour.

Each of the five dysfunctions brings with it an inherent danger for the organization. This is reflected in its structure, systems, co-ordination mechanisms, strategy, decision-making and its ability to change.

When to use it

When confronted with problems, corporate leaders can use this classification of dysfunctions to identify what is wrong with themselves and/or their organizations, and make the necessary adjustments.

Neurotic styles of individuals and organizations

Key factor	Paranoid	Compulsive	Dramatic	Depressive	Schizoid
Characteristics of the dysfunction	■ Suspiciousness ■ Mistrust ■ Hyper-alertness	■ Perfectionism ■ Seeking submission ■ Inability to relax	■ Self-dramatization ■ Narcissistic preoccupation	■ Feeling worthless ■ Loss of motivation	■ Detachment ■ Estrangement ■ Indifference
Core fantasy	■ Cannot trust anyone	■ Must control	■ Want to impress	■ Hopeless	■ Doesn't matter
Dangers	■ Seeking and finding suspicions confirmed	■ Inward orientation ■ Indecisiveness	■ Superficiality	■ Pessimism	■ Frustration with emotional isolation
Organizational focus and structure	■ Organizational intelligence ■ Control structure	■ Information systems for formal control ■ Standardization	■ Bold new ventures ■ Growth ■ Primitive structure	■ Formal routines ■ Hierarchy without leadership	■ Political playground for sub-top
Decision-making	■ Redundant analyses	■ Carefully planned uncertainty reducation	■ Based on hunch, instinct, intuition, etc. ■ Unreflective	■ Tribal battles among sub-top vie for approval by 'leader'	■ Tribal battles among sub-top vie for approval by 'leader'
Power	■ Centralized with top management	■ Top management and corporate staff	■ Narcissistic leader	■ Leadership vacuum	■ Leadership vacuum ■ Shifting coalition

Strategy	■ Risk averse:
	  – reactive
	  – diversification
		■ Planned in detail
		■ Long-term theme
			■ Anything that moves
			■ Corporate wild growth
				■ Aimless
				■ Too busy with petty stuff
					■ Product of individual goals, power and politicking

Change	■ 'Muddling through' ■ Fear of 'leaks'	■ Too rigid for the process of change	■ In defiance of failure, leader fails to bend	■ Meaningful change does not occur	■ Small, incremental ■ Often obstructed

The final analysis

Kets de Vries and Miller have integrated psychiatric and psychological insights with management and organizational behaviour theory to reveal underlying causes of many organizational problems. The real question is whether the 'dysfunctional' will be able to recognize themselves in this model, let alone be willing to consider using it.

Interview with Manfred Kets de Vries: 'A Manager is a Walking Symbol'

By Suzanne Weusten

Manfred Kets de Vries, psychoanalyst, economist and management guru, * *uses models to get a handle on the complicated reality. To change the behaviour of managers, he employs conceptual frameworks such as the 'Triangle of Mental Life' or 'The Five Cs of the Individual Change Process'. His most important model, however, is the 'Neurotic Organizational Model', in which he shows how the personality of the manager infects the culture of the organization: self-awareness is of vital importance to a manager.*

Each year, 20 top-level managers from all over the world come to the European Institute of Business Administration (INSEAD) in Fontainebleau to attend Manfred Kets de Vries' workshop about leadership. They form the inspiration and are the touchstone for his theories about leadership. 'The older people get, the harder it is for them to change. Their parents and teachers have taught them various patterns, which have become ingrained in them over the years. A certain degree of continuity can be found in their behaviour; many people are locked in a mental prison.' In the three weeks that top-level managers follow his workshop, Kets de Vries tries to help them gain personal insight so that they no longer depend on old patterns. 'Mental health means making choices', he says. 'They engage in brief dynamic psychotherapy sessions in a group setting and in an organizational context. Otherwise, they run away.' Indeed, the flexibility to change has diminished in managers who have already lived two-thirds of their life, but Kets de Vries shows them that they still have options.

Manfred Kets de Vries is especially interested in leadership and the psychological processes in organizations. He is the Professor of Leadership Development in the prestigious MBA programme at INSEAD in Fontainebleau. He has written 14 books that have been translated into 12 languages. Some of his publications include The Neurotic Organization, Struggling with the Demon, Life and Death in the Executive Fast Lane. His most recent book is The Leadership Mystique. In addition, he's published almost 200 articles about leadership. Kets de Vries advises top-level managers of companies throughout the entire world, including companies like Goldman Sachs and Nokia.

Leadership and everything related to it fascinates him, especially the neurotic and unhealthy side of it. The idea of 'narcissism' comes up regularly in the conversation. 'Each manager is a narcissist', he declares while gesturing emphatically. 'Each manager also needs a certain dose of narcissism. A problem only arises if narcissism turns into self-conceit, arrogance and hubris.'

Kets de Vries not only likes to talk, but is a quick and lively discussion partner. In his beautiful apartment overlooking the Rive Gauche in Paris, he trips over his words. He gesticulates, stands up, sits down again and, at the same time, is a considerate host. He serves tea with cantuccini and later a glass of white wine with mini pizzas. 'Or would you rather have nuts?', he inquires. His study is filled with rows and rows of books, some can even be found lying under his desk. Recently, his wife bought him a four-volume series of books in Stockholm about Alexander the Great, his latest interest. 'I still have to read this one', he sighs. Mounted on the wall, three stuffed goat heads with big horns look down at us. A hobby, he later explains.

Manfred Kets de Vries calls himself a workaholic. The balance between his work and his private life is completely upset. 'But it doesn't matter', he adds reassuringly. 'The children all moved out long ago.' He works continuously for ten months a year, each day and in the weekend for approximately 80 hours a week. He gets up at 5:00 a.m., writes until about 10:00 a.m., then answers his regular mail and his e-mail and takes care of telephone calls: general garbage, goes to a film and then spends the rest of the day reading or teaching a class. He also likes to work in his second home located in the Alps Maritimes. He actually wrote his last book there. 'In one month', he says proudly. After 10 months he's exhausted and he retreats, preferably into the African wilderness, or to Siberia or Afghanistan. Hunting goats. Kets de Vries loves excitement: 'Thrills and regressions, no sublimations', he laughs.

Excessive Behaviour

'Of course I use models', he says while conjuring up several triangles on his laptop computer. They are as important to him as his cartoons about management, which he has collected over the course of many years. Just as models simplify the complicated reality, cartoons support his theories with humour.

The core of Kets de Vries' work is also his most important model: the *neurotic organizational model*. The basic assumption here is that the strategy and structure of an organization can actually be influenced by the personality of the manager. The stronger the CEO's personality, the more his way of acting will be reflected in the culture, structure and strategy of the company. The neurotic organizational model identifies five types of organizations and management styles: the paranoid, the compulsive, the dramatic, the depressive, and the schizoid (see box, p. 151).

'The basic idea', he says, 'is that organizations are originally good, but they are ruined by the excessive behaviour of the managing director. Naturally, this is stereotyping since most managing directors use a mix of styles. What I am trying to say, however, is that we make managing directors too important. We say that *he* does things, that it is *his* fault and that something is the way it is because of *him*. Alexander the Great did not fight alone in Asia for four years. There were more people involved'.

In his leadership workshop, Kets de Vries encourages participants to change. 'Change is not a simple process, nor is it a comfortable one, he says, and senior managers prefer then not to change. They remain locked into their dysfunctional behaviour, they avoid conflicts and are concerned about the details instead of the big picture.' In order to break their entrenched behaviour patterns and to instil a sense of self-awareness (the most important characteristic for a manager), he asks them unorthodox questions: 'In order to know how successful managers can increase their effectiveness, we have to immerse ourselves more in their mental life. What really motivates them? Why do they behave like this?'

'The *triangle of mental life* is a model that can help us understand someone's psychological make-up. The three corners of this model are behaviour, emotions and cognitions. In order to change, people have to be affected in their head and in their heart. They have to understand cognitively why a certain change is advantageous to them, and they also have to be affected emotionally.'

According to Kets de Vries, you can easily overlook the relationship between emotion and cognition. As a consultant, he discovered during his conversations with top-level managers that they were often in complete agreement with him, but still failed to change. He had to reach them in another way. For example, there was a banker who withdrew when faced with difficult situations and reacted in a way that was cold and detached. This man was only able to change his behaviour after having been confronted with a letter from his 19-year-old daughter who described how difficult it was for her having a father that was sometimes so inaccessible.

Another model that Kets de Vries uses is the *five Cs of the individual change process*. Change begins with *concern*, with daily problems and frustrations and with negative emotions. The workshop participants are challenged to overcome their frustrations and aversions and to discover their central management style. This can happen by means of *confrontation* in the group in the form of questions and comments. Afterwards, the process of *clarification* follows: a consequence of the earlier confrontation. By associating and by establishing a relationship between the current and previous behavioural patterns, the participant gains insight into his behaviour and can then formulate what he wants to change. Take the detached banker as an example. After the direct confrontation with the letter from his daughter, he was able to consider the causes of his aloofness and feel the need to do something about it. The fourth C, the *crystallization*, is an inner journey to gain more self-knowledge. Lastly, the internalization of a new mind-set is the *change*.

Self-awareness and Empathy

According to Kets de Vries, 'A manager is more than the lonely man at the top with a vision. Nowadays, he is also the coach, the chief storyteller, the actor and the teddy bear'. In the last 20 years, leadership has become hugely complicated. The lifecycle of top-level managers is much shorter than in the past. If managing directors used to work for a company for an average 20 years, they now average only five years before they are off to the next job. 'That isn't good', he says. 'If you want to change a company, you need at least five years. And if you are the managing director for only a short period of time, you cannot see what you are doing. It is very difficult to make good investments for the long term, if you are constantly feeling pressure from the shareholders.'

Managing directors need to be able to do more than just look far into the future and have a helicopter view of things. They also have to cope with an information overdose.

'I used to work for Goldman Sachs; there were managers there who received 300 e-mails and voice-mails daily. You have to be good at time management and at delegating things, otherwise you won't make it. I advised them to make a simple matrix, a model: fun and not fun, necessary and not necessary. Do things which clearly have added value and which are fun and necessary. And every once in awhile do fun things which are not necessary. I call that banana time.' Kets de Vries, too, struggles with an information overload. 'My days are getting longer and longer, I have more and more things to do and I'm not very good at saying no.'

Even if managing directors are making the correct financial decisions and holding out against the overwhelming amount of information, they're still not there yet. Their social and emotional qualities are next, and according to Kets de Vries, these are the most important. He lists three: self-awareness, empathy, and the ability to rename things positively. 'Self-awareness is of vital importance to a manager. One of the managing directors from my workshop is such a self-conscious type. 'Each morning when I get to work I can make 10,000 people unhappy', he says. He knows that he has this power and he handles it carefully. 'As a manager you are a walking symbol and you have to be aware of that constantly.'

Managers can also use symbols to manipulate things; that strengthens their power and their standing. 'After crossing the Hellespont, Alexander the Great jabbed his spear into the ground and declared: "*Now I take possession of Asia*".' However narcissistic the man was, with such dramatic and symbolic statements he did write history, and he anchored memories in a collective consciousness.

Self-awareness also means that managers have to be aware of their strengths and weaknesses. 'Richard Branson, top man at the Virgin Group (UK), doesn't know much about accountancy. But he knows that about himself, and also knows that it doesn't matter. He just makes sure that he has a good accountant.'

Nolan's IT growth stages

The big idea

Nolan's (1979) theory of organizational data processing (DP) growth distinguishes a number of phases in the development of information technology (IT):

- initiation
- contagion/expansion
- control
- integration
- data administration/architecture
- maturity and de-concentration.

Nolan argues that there are specific, identifiable issues peculiar to each phase. The range of issues applies to all organizational aspects of IT: information systems, users, technology, IT specialists' management tools, etc. Each phase should be managed differently, so as to balance the so-called 'IT growth processes'. Some of these processes relate to supply, others to demand.

When to use it

The first step in using the model is the process of identifying the stage of development of the organization. This is often one of the most valuable processes, because it develops understanding of IT issues in a broader sense. Nolan offers benchmarks for stage identification at two levels.

The first level deals with quantifiable aspects related to DP expenditure. The expenditure benchmark is based on the premise that DP spending either equals, outpaces, or lags behind the organization's sales

	Phase 1 Initiation	Phase 2 Expansion	Phase 3 Control	Phase 4 Integration	Phase 5 Architecture	Phase 6 Deconcentration
Characteristics						
Applications portfolio	■ Functional cost reduction applications	■ Proliferation	■ Upgrade documentation application restructure	■ Retrofitting with data base technology	■ Organizational data integration	■ Application and data integration, mirroring data flows
DP/IT organization	■ Specialization for technological learning	■ User-oriented programmers	■ Middle management	■ Establish computer utility and user account teams	■ Data administration	■ Data resource management
Planning control	■ Lax	■ More lax	■ Formalized planning and control	■ Tailored planning and control systems	■ Shared data and common systems	■ Data resource strategic planning
User awareness	■ 'Hands off'	■ Superficially enthusiastic	■ Arbitrarily held accountable	■ Accountability learning	■ Effectively accountable	■ Joint responsibility data processing and users
Benchmarks Expenditure	■ Tracks sales growth rate	■ Exceeds sales growth rate	■ Growing at lower than sales growth rate	■ Exceeds sales growth rate	■ Growing at lower than sales growth rate	■ Tracks sales growth rate
Technology	■ 100% batch processing	■ 80% batch, 20% remote job entry	■ 70% batch, 15% database, 10% inquiry and 5% time-sharing processing	■ Half batch/job entry, other half mainly database and data communication	■ Less than 20% batch/job entry, mostly data communication	■ Even less batch job, while increasing use of microprocessing

Applications porfolio	■ Concentration on labour-intensive automation, scientific support and clerical replacement	■ Applications moving to user locations for data generation and data use	■ Balance between central system and decentralized user application
DP/IT organization	■ Centralized processing, operating as a closed shop	■ Data processing becomes data custodian. Computer utility established and achieves reliability	■ Organization data resource management with responsibility layers
Planning and control	■ Internal planning & control. Standardization in programming, responsibility accounting and project management.	■ External planning & control to manage data resources. Value-added user charge-back, steering commitee and data administration	
User awarness	■ Reactive user. Superficial involvement	■ End user is driving force, responsible for data quality and value-added use	■ End user is driving force, responsible for data quality and value-added use

growth, depending on its growth stage (see model illustration). The IT benchmark is based on various data processing statistics.

Second-level analysis delves deeper into qualitative aspects that describe the phases, such as applications portfolio, organization, planning, control and user awareness.

The next steps in managing growth of DP/IT, according to Nolan are:

1. Recognize the fundamental transition of the organisation's DP/IT developmental stages.
2. Recognize the importance of enabling technologies.
3. Identify developmental stages per operating unit.
4. Develop a multi-level strategy and plan.
5. Make the steering committee work.

The final analysis

Nolan's model reflects on one of the major problems associated with the development and deployment of IT in an organization: varying expectations, different levels of maturity and lack of co-ordination between users and providers of IT. The necessity of fitting demand and supply is of paramount importance. The clear distinction and specific description of different stages of IT development in an organization have contributed to the great popularity of Nolan's model.

However, in spite of the clarity of the basic principles of matching growth processes and development stages, i.e. ensuring a fit between supply and demand, the model tends to get complicated when applied to a real situation. Analyses are frequently so sophisticated that results and specific actions are not easily understood, let alone implemented.

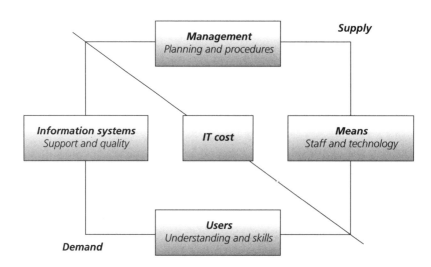

Overhead value analysis

The big idea

Overhead value analysis (OVA) focuses on optimising the effectiveness of indirect activities and services in an organization. OVA makes explicit and compares the costs of the indirect activities with the resulting output of the primary processes they support.

OVA can be used to slash and reorganize overhead activities, both as a pre-emptive and as a last resort measure. The desired result does not necessarily limit itself to lowering cost; many organizations simply want to increase awareness of service demands for the internal customer. It goes without saying that OVA has a significant impact on the people employed in the indirect activities under scrutiny.

The client, a manufacturer of military and advanced remote control technology, saw slowing financial results and lack of organizational versatility as early signs of a need to reassess its indirect organizational functions.

The OVA team set out to identify overhead activities and made an orderly list of activities and costs. A decision was then made to further engage in a full OVA project in order to restructure the organization and drastically reduce the number of indirect functions.

The result was a transformation from a functional organization to a market-driven business unit structure: departments delivered value to their internal customers, and many tasks that were formerly divided among primary and secondary functions were decentralized. The change process enjoyed wide support within the organization, as all parties involved felt that they were participating in their own 'reinvention'.

When to use it

For any OVA project to succeed, the success factors are as follows:

- Organizational objectives are known.
- The organizational structure is in place.
- The scope of OVA is determined.
- No other projects are interfered with or otherwise disrupt the OVA.
- There is sufficient support throughout the organization.

Typically, there are six basic steps for an overhead value analysis.
The first step is to **create a foundation**. This includes three sub-steps:

1. Define output as demanded.
2. Determine required activities.
3. Identify and assess the end product.

The second step is to make an **orderly listing of activities and costs**. This step includes:

1. estimating costs of input/resources
2. estimating costs of activities
3. allocating cost to products (ABC).

Thirdly, get a (internal) **customer evaluation** of the service and output. Relevant aspects are necessity (e.g. critical, desired or nice-to-have), quality, quantity and cost. Customers are asked for both an assessment of the current output and indications as to what improvements must be made. Both interviews and questionnaires are used in the evaluation.

Having identified possible improvements, the OVA team must, in step four, **identify cost-saving opportunities**. This forces the organization to make a statement with regard to priorities for output and required activities. The actual quantitative objective is not necessarily the result of a calculated improvement potential, but must viewed as challenging yet achievable with the new work method(s).

Next, **prioritize opportunities** with the help of the four elements used earlier in the customer evaluation:

- Necessity: is value added?
- Is quality of output sufficient?
- Is quantity of output sufficient?
- Can it be done at reasonable cost?

Overlapping the identification and prioritization of opportunities is the question of whether or not to eliminate, change, automate, integrate and/or outsource certain activities. This is very much a pragmatic process executed by management in conjunction with experts and managers of the overhead departments.

A project in itself, the sixth and final step is to **implement** the set of changes discussed and decided upon in the former five steps.

The final analysis

The results of an OVA analysis are often presented in numbers, whereas most of the data gathering is in fact qualitative. The data are usually directly or indirectly provided by the very people whose jobs are 'on the line'. This calls for benchmarks to verify the data given.

Potential pitfalls of OVA are:

- insufficient data and information
- insufficient support for results and arguments
- insufficient support for implementation.

Both management and analysts should make the process as easy as possible for the subjects. Getting everybody involved to a point where plans are perceived to be self-made is a major contribution to the potential success of OVA.

OVA is often used in combination with *activity-based costing*. As we have already said, the implementation phase should be viewed as a change management project in its own right.

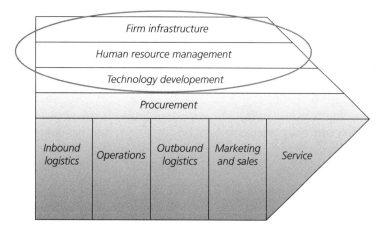

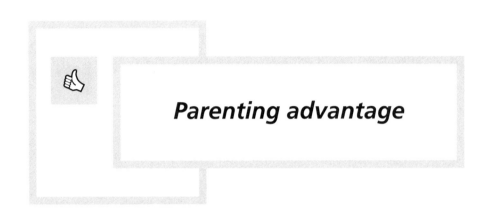

Parenting advantage

The big idea

The purpose of the parenting advantage model is to determine the conditions under which corporate parent companies can create most value.

Goold, Campbell and Alexander (1994) argue that there are four main sorts of value creation open to the parent company, each with potential complications that may also result in value destruction:

1. **Stand-alone influence**. The parent enhances the stand-alone performance of each individual business unit through monitoring of key targets, approving major capital expenses and bringing in talented top management. But value may also be destroyed. What does the parent's management know better in 10 per cent of its time than business unit management in 100 per cent of its time? This is the '10 per cent versus 100 per cent' paradox.

2. **Linkage influence**. Parents create value by enhancing linkages between business units. Corporate synergetic processes, transfer pricing and even personal networking encourage value-enhancing relationships that would otherwise not have existed.

3. **Central functions and services**. Enforced by the chief executive and other senior line managers, the parent offers a range of corporate functions, providing functional leadership and cost-effective services in addition to creating stand-alone and linkage influence. Large overheads, bureaucracy and ineffectiveness lead many corporate functions to absorb as much, if not more, value than they create. These functions must compete with external specialists to prevent their 'downsizing'.

4. **Corporate development**. The parent buys, develops and sells businesses and corporate ventures. Value is created as well as destroyed depending upon the quality of valuations acquisition targets and spin-offs. Funds can be funnelled to losing ventures, and potentially successful ventures may dry up.

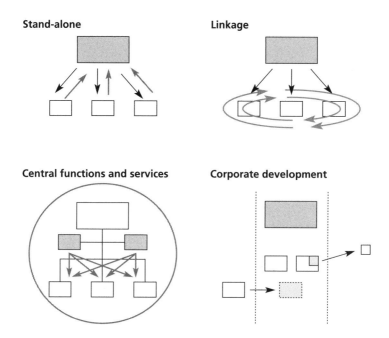

Which type of influence is best to create value as a parent can be determined depending and based upon certain conditions related to paradoxes of parenting advantage. These paradoxes more or less evolve around contradicting forces: costs versus benefits, control versus empowerment, protectionism versus market strength, etc.

When to use it

In order to create parenting advantage, corporate strategists must understand characteristics of the parent, the business(es) it owns, its relative strength, and how this may evolve in the future.

The characteristics of the parent can be audited through five inter-related lenses:

- mental maps
- functions, central services, and resources

- decentralization contracts
- people and skills
- parenting structures, systems and processes.

Understanding the parent's characteristics therefore requires looking into the company's values and behaviour, and where they came from. What roles did the parent traditionally play? Do people in the business unit still see the parent in an 'old' way? How does the parent interact with its businesses? And at the end of all this: what is the cost to the parent?

The portfolio of business units is the corporate strategist's next agenda point toward defining parenting advantage opportunities. Issues are:

- scope and definition of each business unit
- performance and measurement
- likely nature and impact of parenting/deparenting opportunities
- distinguishing stand-alone value-creating opportunities from parenting opportunities
- quantifying each opportunity.

Opportunities are to found in several areas, including scale, management, risk-taking, expertise, relationships, linkages, decision-making, as well as many more.

Understanding critical success factors in the relationship between parent and business unit, especially those related to performance measurement and decision-making, is the third key step in assessing parenting advantage opportunities. Beyond this, the parent's potential impact on all areas of the business should be analysed, including other units.

Corporate strategy changes affect both parent and portfolio. Assessing the fit helps to identify likely change areas:

- Do the parent and the business see the same opportunities?
- Does the parent have any obviously highly effective characteristics to create value?
- Are there issues with key success factors?

Additionally, Goold, Campbell and Alexander advise upon the need for and approach to analysing rival parent companies, together with whom a business could potentially create as much or more value.

Finally, a vision of the future using scenario modelling techniques (see Scenario planning, later in this book) will help the parent to judge its ability to succeed under other circumstances. Assessing the appropriate parent roles in different scenarios and securing strategic options to generate value in multiple ways is a time-consuming, but worthwhile task.

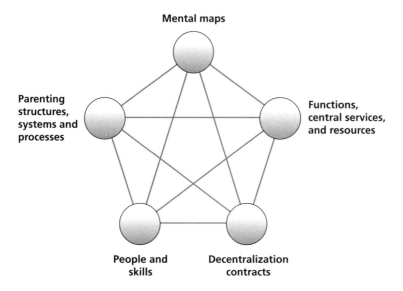

Mental maps

Parenting structures, systems and processes

Functions, central services, and resources

People and skills

Decentralization contracts

The final analysis

The parenting advantage framework helps corporate management to rethink 'naturally grown corporate structures' and the very reason for existence of the corporate parent.

The four value-creating opportunities can be difficult to apply in practice, due to their strong dependence upon situational characteristics. They are, furthermore, not mutually exclusive, with potential overlap in the value created.

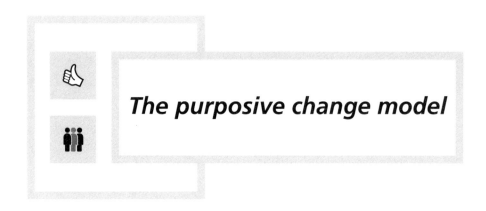

The purposive change model

The big idea

General managers are responsible for 'everything' in a company. An important task for general management is therefore the design and realization of strategic organizational changes. General managers have to ask themselves how the right things can be done well in order to achieve the company's objectives. Following Bower (2000) this is the domain of purposive change: 'what it should be and how it should be accomplished'. Accomplishment in this case refers to the achievements of general managers in their role as organization builders, architects or designers. Related is the question of how managers can create the right conditions for the realization of aims, i.e. how they can ensure that organizations are arranged in such a way that they function properly.

Based on an in-depth study of companies like ST Microelectronics, Nokia and Sollac, all three winners of the European Quality Award, ten Have, ten Have and Stevens (2001) developed the *purposive change model*. Integrated congruency is the key concept in this model and is interpreted as 'having everything fit together organizationally'. More specifically, 'integrated' refers to all the issues, components and disciplines the general manager has to deal with. 'Congruent' means that the various components must be in harmony organizationally and work towards the same goals.

The study of the companies mentioned resulted in the identification and description of four general management processes which, taken together, form the basis of a distinctive way of organizing: direction, consistency, coherence and feedback. Organizational change is seen as the product of these management processes.

- Direction – refers to the organization's choices and common aims, including its mission and corporate values.

- Consistency – predominantly the vertical translation of the common aim and organizational values into objectives, tasks and behavioural standards (*vertical fit*).
- Coherence – relates to the horizontal co-ordination between processes, chains, operating companies, departments and individuals, and also includes structures, systems and competencies (*horizontal fit*).
- Feedback – refers to the arrangement of an organization in such a way that learning can take place at all levels within varying time-frames.

Direction, consistency and coherence have a stabilising effect, whereas feedback is more dynamic. Goal-oriented, purposive change can be achieved by shaping the four management processes of direction, consistency, coherence and feedback and the underlying elements and resources, into an integrated, interactive whole.

When to use it

The purposive change model and its underlying management processes can be set in motion by translating them into concrete management actions and interventions. How this can be done is illustrated by describing some of the practices of the companies studied.

Direction is determined by formulating an explicit, comprehensive long-term management philosophy. Senior management must be completely committed to this philosophy. Moreover, senior management must be able, in particular, to communicate constantly and openly about the philosophy.

Consistency can be promoted by formulating the company strategy and change objectives for the whole organization and then translating these into concrete aims and activities. This process can be supported by the translation of the corporate values so that the operationalization of goals and style and behaviour are combined.

Coherence is created by organizing operating processes and functional work areas together. By doing this all facets of the company can be harmonized with each other. To this end, business strategy and change objectives must be translated into a limited number of key processes and a hierarchy of operating processes based on them.

Feedback is expressed through infrastructure created specifically for the purpose, and is provided by regular, company-wide measurement and targeted reward of performances that contribute to the achievement of company strategy and change objectives.

The final analysis

The purposive change model and its main principle of integrated congruency state that the better the fit organizationally, the more effective an organization will be in the realization of its ambition and goals. The most

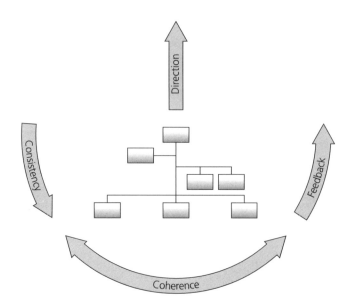

important comments have to do with the main focus of the model, situations in which it will be effective and aspects which are not highlighted by the model.

Though the model provides ways of communicating a direction and setting the wheels in motion for its realization, it is not equipped to establish the *content* of the said direction, i.e. the ambition and goals. Establishing a strategy, developing a business model and assessing strategic options all demand their own processes, to which end a multitude of other models have been developed. The purposive change model's main focus is to translate and implement the outcomes of such processes by arranging the organization in a way that will facilitate the achievement of its goals. Doing this takes time and requires a high degree of discipline, time and persistence, as is shown by organizations like Nokia and ST Microelectronics.

The model has proven to work in both dynamic and stable industries, but is based on the principle of *minimum crisis – maximum change – maximum management commitment*. Starting from a minimum crisis situation, in which the company has a number of strategic options and possibilities in terms of the allocation of people and resources, it can create maximum change under the condition of maximum management commitment. The purposive change model is not a model for *maximum crisis situations* in which interventions are focused on the short term and geared towards immediate financial results. Furthermore, the model largely ignores the more emotional, irrational and creative processes in an organization. It does not deny that such processes exist, but neither does it provide insights with regard to their characteristics. It simply tries to develop ways of organizing in which they and their outcomes can be countered or embedded.

Risk reward analysis

The big idea

The risk reward analysis charts potential rewards of strategic options against the associated risk level. The result is an assessment of the attractiveness of strategic options, serving as a basis on which to make strategic decisions for resource allocation.

When to use it

The risk reward analysis can be performed at any level of detail: the CEO could do it on the back of an envelope, or he might ask a team of analysts to perform a full-fledged analysis, including extensive market assessments, ROI calculations, scenario development and sensitivity analyses. The fundamental steps remain the same, however.

Management and/or analysts should determine a list of viable strategic options and their potential rewards. For example, options may be international market development, new product introduction, outsourcing manufacturing, etc. The additional savings and/or reduced costs and investments represent a potential reward that can be quantified. Additionally, the attractiveness might be scored based on qualitative factors, such as expansion of long-term strategic freedom, build-up of capabilities in an emerging technology, etc.

For each option, a thorough analysis must then be carried out to assess the risk associated with the option. Factors to consider in this respect are: level of investment, industry threats, cut-off from other options, etc.

The final analysis

One of the most prevailing pitfalls in strategic management is that decisions are made with limited information and lack of multiple perspectives. Rosy predictions about the potential rewards of strategic options push risk analysis into the background. Though potentially tainted by the same cloud of optimism, the risk reward analysis at least draws the subject of risk forward once.

The problem with this model is that valuations of both dimensions, risk and reward, are the result of a complex integration of subsets of factors. How each factor weighs in and interrelates with others can therefore be affected by emotions.

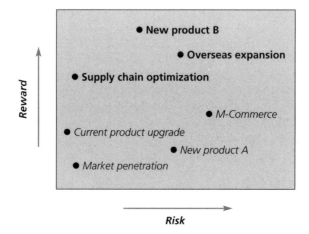

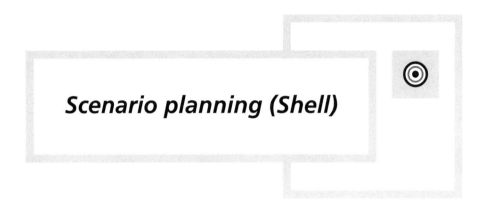

Scenario planning (Shell)

The big idea

Traditionally, planning was based on forecasts. The problem with fore-
casting is that it is based on the assumption that the current state of
affairs will remain the same – as soon as the business environment loses
its stability, forecasts become unreliable. They thus fail just when they are
needed most, often with disastrous results. Faced with raging instability
in the oil industry in the mid-1970s, after two decades of relative calm,
planners at Shell went in search of an alternative, more effective way of
preparing for the future. The result was *scenario planning*.

Instead of preparing for the future by assuming that it will resemble
the present, the type of scenario planning developed at Shell is built
around the assumption that the business environment *will* change.
Rather than trying to remove uncertainty, the challenge is to accept and
try to understand it. The aim is not necessarily to 'get it right' but to illu-
minate the major forces driving the system, their interrelationships and
the critical uncertainties.

Scenarios structure the future into predetermined and uncertain elements. By identifying and exploring predetermined elements – events
that have already been set in motion, interdependencies, breaks in trends
– it is possible to devote more attention to the uncertain elements, i.e. the
possible consequeces of the predetermined events. This in turn allows a
number of scenarios to be developed.

One of the critical success factors is the removal of the crisis of perception from which many managers suffer: the inability to see an emerging
novel reality by being locked inside obsolete assumptions. To quote
Drucker: 'The greatest danger in times of turbulence is not the turbulence; it is to act with yesterday's logic'. It is therefore vital to penetrate
the microcosm of decision-makers, making them question their assumptions about the way their business world works, and getting them to
reorganize their own inner models of reality.

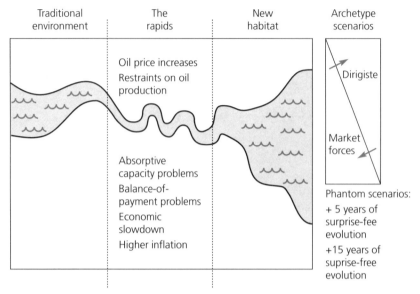

| Traditional environment | The rapids | New habitat | Archetype scenarios |

Oil price increases
Restraints on oil production

Dirigiste

Market forces

Absorptive capacity problems
Balance-of-payment problems
Economic slowdown
Higher inflation

Phantom scenarios:
+ 5 years of surprise-fee evolution
+15 years of suprise-free evolution

Source: adapted from Wack (1985a)

When to use it

The creation of scenarios effectively organizes a tangle of seemingly unrelated economic, technological, political and social information, transforming it into a framework for judgment. Scenario planning thus has a protective role, enabling organizations to anticipate and understand risk. There is also an entrepreneurial aspect, in that it can help bring to light new strategic options.

The process of constructing scenarios can be divided into three main sections:

- Identification and analysis of the predetermined elements – what events are taking place, which trends are emerging that will have an impact on your business? At this stage you do not have to know when or where such developments will take effect, only that they are definitely happening.

- Charting of the interrelationships – what is the likely combined effect on your operating environment?

- Development of scenarios depending on the resulting uncertainties – ideally three, with four as an absolute maximum. Bear in mind that it is dangerous to present three scenarios describing outcomes along a single dimension, because people cannot resist seeing the middle one as some sort of baseline; likewise, two tend to push people to choose for a happy medium.

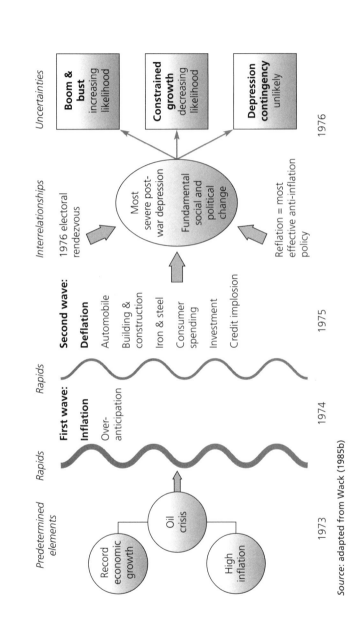

Source: adapted from Wack (1985b)

Scenarios are generally most effective when combined with:

- Strategic vision – you must have a clear, structured view of what you want your organization to be before you start, as opposed to what you want it to do;
- Option planning – if no new strategic options result, then the scenario creation process has not worked.

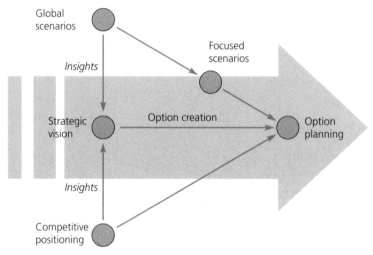

Source: adapted from Wack (1985b)

The final analysis

How convenient it would be to be able to predict the future! Unfortunately, scenario planning is far from being a modern day crystal ball. There is no way to simplify the complexity of the future, it being the result of countless combinations of uncertainties. All scenario planning can do is help managers to cope with the complexity by offering them ways to structure their thinking.

Scenario planning is a lengthy process, generally being conducted over a number of years. Furthermore, there is absolutely no way of seeing whether it was useful until long after the event. With hindsight there are two questions that can and should be asked to judge whether or not it worked. If done correctly, scenario planning should warn of all major events that happen. The first question is thus: what, if anything, was left out? The next question is: did it lead to action? Planning is after all, nothing more than speculation unless managers ultimately act other than in the past.

Rather than being an event that takes place on a one-off basis when times get really tough, scenario planning should be considered as ongoing training in awareness and flexibility. By constantly scanning the environment, assessing the potential impact of likely events, and ensuring that the organization is in a position to cope with and preferably benefit from them, the likelihood of long-term survival can be greatly increased.

Schools of strategy synthesis

The big idea

The strategy field is littered with theories and methodologies alike: core competencies, complexity, game theory, hypercompetition, knowledge-based competition, and so on. Some organizational scientists argue that strategy is a science of fashion.

Elfring and Volberda (2001) believe that it is about time to focus. A development of the strategy field along the lines of so-called synthesizing schools would make the field less vulnerable to fragmentation and provide a solid foundation for the accumulation of new insights. The three proposed synthesizing schools are:

- the boundary school – pondering the issues of where to draw the boundary of an organization and how to manage across the divide;
- the dynamic capability school – regarding strategic management as a collective learning process aimed at developing distinctive capabilities that are difficult to copy;
- the configuration school – viewing strategy as a process of emerging and declining strategic organizational configurations, such as strategy modes, archetypes and developmental stages.

The schools are not mutually exclusive, but highly complementary. Elfring and Volberda use four core dimensions of the field of strategy to 'measure' the ability of the three schools to deal with the differentiation-integration tension:

- domain of inquiry
- contribution of base disciplines
- methodological approach
- purpose of the inquiry.

	Boundary school	Dynamic capability school	Configuration school
Issues	■ Make or buy? ■ Outsourcing ■ Vertical integration ■ Partner selection ■ Own or share?	■ 'Compete with what?' ■ Ability to use resources ■ Creating and/or acquiring new abilities to use resources ■ How substantial is the advantage?	■ Emerging and declining strategic organizational configurations ■ Organizational typologies ■ Contingencies of configurations ■ Control v. flexibility
Mandatory theory and buzz words	■ Transaction cost economics ■ Asset management and control ■ Strategy v. commodity approach ■ Network organization ■ Tacit knowledge transfer	■ Resource-based theory of the film ■ Organizational learning ■ Core competencies ■ Value disciplines	■ Co-ordinated mechanisms ■ Growth stages ■ Organizational life cycle ■ Strategic archetypes ■ Organizational dimensions
Tools, tips and take-aways	■ Divide activities into strategic and non-strategic ■ Out-of-hand often means out-of-head: loss of informal shared understanding as a result of outsourcing ■ There is no best way, and even if there was, it would change with time. Trust is (still) the first key to healthy alliances ■ Aliances make firms more dependent upon other firms to develop competitiveness	■ Given time, distinct capabilities tend to lose their distinctiveness and competitive edge ■ Dynamic capabilities remain valuable as long as competitive change persists – and it always does ■ The only certainty is uncertainty ■ The only thing that stays the same is the fact that everything changes ■ There are different levels of organizational learning, most notably individual v. collective	■ There is no one best configuration: there are too many situational characteristics ■ There is no escaping the age-old dilemma of centralized control v. flexibility. At best, an organization can strive to capture the best of both worlds ■ Contingent explanations of effective strategy configurations run the risk of exponential complexity, outstripping this school of the very essence of its teachings: to create a model for an organization.
Direction	■ Historically too static. ■ More dynamic interorganizational relationship theories and tools are expected	■ Most research efforts rooted in stability ■ New research focuses on the dynamics of capability development	■ Focus traditionally on cognitive simplification and psychological closure ■ More empirical research is needed

Synthesis is less far-reaching than integration: the different theories can be seen as complementary without the need to either fully agree or disagree.

When to use it

Elfring and Volberda drew up a framework to encourage organizational scientists and managers to focus their research efforts. For the every-day manager, this framework can be of help when it comes to placing another concept, idea or management fad in a familiar perspective.

The final analysis

Elfring and Volberda have made an impressive, seemingly exhaustive, yet complex approach to create focus in the field of strategy. On the one hand, it is valuable to be able to cluster strategy approaches; on the other hand, there seems to be no escaping from the fundamental issues that underpin the wild growth of strategy concepts:

- too many interrelations and interdependencies
- too many different perspectives
- too many difficult words
- too many literature references.

Bear in mind that gurus are not going to build on, and within the constraints of, any strategy synthesis framework; they are far more likely to build from scratch or, quite shamelessly, create buzzwords for issues that Elfring and Volberda have included in their framework.

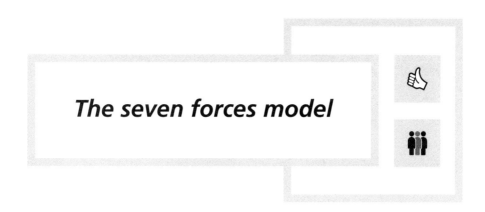

The seven forces model

The big idea

Many, if not all, change processes fail in the absence of urgency, vision, infrastructure, know-how, and co-ordination. Based on client case studies, Berenschot (1991) devised the *seven forces model*, outlining the seven forces that make things happen:

- **necessity** – a shock to break the inertia and to create a sense of urgency;
- **vision** – specific images in order to make people 'see' what is requested of them;
- **success** – early successes that create a sense of confirmation the new way is 'better';
- **spirit** – the power and strength to initiate and maintain a high level of commitment;
- **structure** – structural support at organizational level to challenge people, as well as to endorse the changes;
- **capabilities** – knowledge, skills and empowerment to balance the new tasks and responsibilities;
- **systems** – information, reviews and rewards to close the loop and confirm desired performance.

Although the seven forces are most effective when applied integrally, they serve different roles in realizing change.

- Necessity, vision and success provide the organization with a sense of purpose in its change efforts. These forces are like stories: awakening, confrontational, and illustrating. Key aspects are opportunities and threats, as well as inspiration and a sense of 'being in this together'.

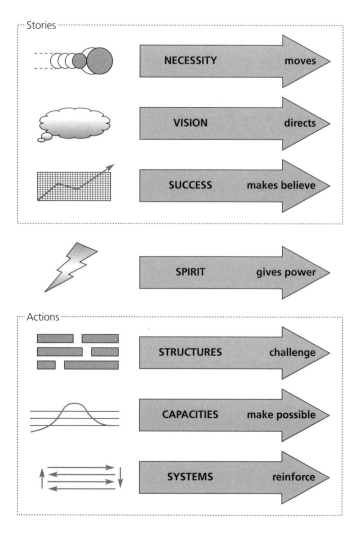

- Structures, capabilities and systems require action for very specific changes in the organization's 'hard' elements structure and systems, as well as (human) competencies.
- Spirit is a process power that fuels all other six forces.

When to use it

The model is primarily used to help understand the necessary elements and structure of a change process. Necessity can be the result either of a situation with which the organization is confronted with (e.g. cash crisis), or of a deliberate action by management or change agents (e.g. announcing major lay-offs). More often than not, necessity has to be brought to the organization's attention by external parties, such as investors and unions. Consultants often serve to articulate the necessity, pinpointing what the key issues are. However, the messenger is often mistaken for the perpetrator and may be confronted with denial, aggression and even anger. Therefore, a deliberate action to create awareness of necessity should never be used in isolation: one has to present a way out of the mess.

The final analysis

The leader must show spirit and have visible faith in the future, despite the dire state of the organization. For that kind of spirit, the leader needs to create a vision for his followers. In order to convince the new followers, there must be early proof of success of the new vision.

Without the means to create early success, there will be a meagre following. The newly spirited organization needs to be able to achieve its vision with proper resources, using effective systems and efficient structures.

The primary aim of the seven forces model is to bring order to the relevant forces in the organizational change process. The power of the model lies in its simplicity, but one must take care not to forget that oversimplification may obscure the complex field of behavioural and organizational principles and design. Successful application of the model requires further investigation into these very areas.

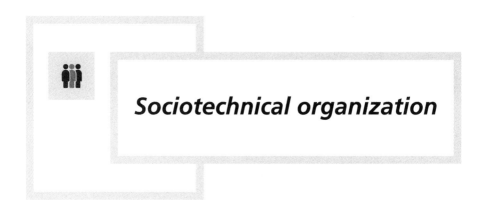

Sociotechnical organization

The big idea

Sociotechnical organization design is based on the premise that both social and technological elements determine the productivity of a group or even an entire organization: a more meaningful work environment can thus increase employee motivation.

One key factor is that a group should be organized so as to increase participation in the group effort. Sociotechnical organization design thus minimizes task splitting. On the contrary, the scope of tasks for each individual should be widened to create a need and drive for learning and sense of purpose. An individual's ability to perform a multitude of tasks increases the flexibility, sustainability and independence of a group. Of major importance are the internal and external degrees of freedom:

- internal freedom to perform multiple tasks according to a work method chosen by the group or individual;
- external freedom to influence the work flow around the group (either within the organization or in its direct environment).

Another essential factor is technology. Rather than being used to simplify human tasks, technology should be applied to improve the work environment, allowing employees to experience a greater sense of purpose.

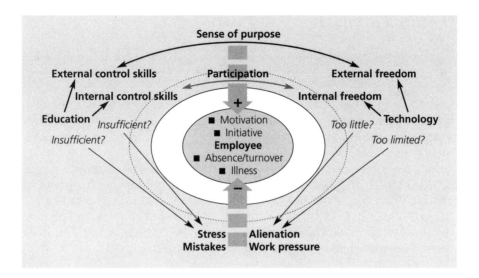

When to use it

Taylor and Felton (1993) propose four practical phases to redesign the organization:

1. **Discovery**:
   - education on sociotechnical system design
   - project planning
   - management commitment
   - project start-up issues.

2. **Systems understanding**:
   - create steering and study groups
   - plan and implement diagnostic methods
   - analyse environment, technical and social subsystems.

3. **Creating the ideal organization**:
   - involve constituents in redesign
   - test alternative designs against goals
   - create provisional design.

4. **Implementation**:
   - planning
   - involvement of people affected
   - operational design
   - evaluation and fine-tuning.

The final analysis

The various phases and elements involved in sociotechnical organization and systems design each contribute to a more productive workforce both individually and as a whole.

Sociotechnical organization design was originally intended for production organization environments, but has found its way in other organizations, too: services, education, government, logistics/transportation, financial/insurance.

Sociotechnical organization design tends to focus most on organizational structuring, even though it was primarily intended for the combination of people, structures and technology. The human factor is often catered to merely because of the participation factor and the importance of a sense of purpose. Considerable attention must be paid to the human factor if tangible benefits are to be gained from this approach.

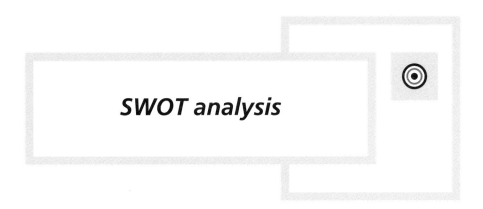

SWOT analysis

The big idea

Any company undertaking strategic planning will at some point assess its strengths and weaknesses. When combined with an inventory of opportunities and threats in (or even beyond) the company's external environment, the company is effectively making what is called a SWOT analysis: establishing its current position in the light of its *strengths*, *weaknesses*, *opportunities* and *threats*.

When to use it

The first step in carrying out a SWOT analysis is to identify the said strengths, weaknesses, opportunities and threats. It is important to note that strengths and weaknesses are intrinsic (potential) value creating skills or assets, or the lack thereof, relative to competitive forces. Opportunities and threats, however, are external factors: they are not created by the company, but emerge as a result of the competitive dynamics caused by (future) 'gaps' or 'crunches' in the market.

Strengths

What is the company really good at? Do we benefit from an experienced sales force, or easy access to raw materials? Do people buy our products (partly) because of our brand(s) or reputation? Strengths are *not*: a growing market, new products, etc.

Weaknesses

Though weaknesses are often seen as the logical 'inverse' of the company's threats, the company's lack of strength in a particular discipline or market is not necessarily a relative weakness, providing (potential) competitors lack this particular strength as well.

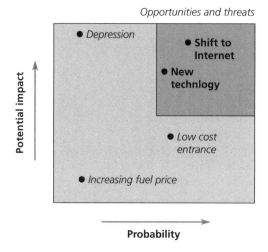

Strengths and weaknesses can be measured in an internal or external audit, for example, through benchmarking (see Benchmarking model).

Opportunities and threats occur as a result of external macroenvironmental forces such as demographic, economic, technological, political, legal, social and cultural dynamics, as well as external industry-specific environmental forces such as customers, competitors, distribution channels and suppliers.

Opportunities

Are any technological developments or demographic changes taking place, or could demand for your products or services increase as a result of successful partnerships? Can you perhaps use assets in other ways, introduce your current products in new markets or turn R&D into cash by licensing concepts, technologies or selling patents? There are many opportunities. The level of detail and (perceived) degree of realism determine the extent of opportunity analysis.

Threats

Your competitor's opportunity may well be a threat to you. Also, changes in regulations, substitute technologies and other forces in the competitive field may pose serious threats to your company: lower sales, higher cost of operations, higher cost of capital, inability to make break-even, shrinking margins or profitability, rates of return dropping significantly below market expectations, etc.

Both opportunities and threats can be classified according to their potential impact and actual probability, as illustrated below.

	Strengths (S)	Weaknesses (W)
Opportunities (O)	■ **SO Strategies** *Use strengths to take advantage of opportunities*	■ **WO Strategies** *Take advantage of opportunities by overcoming weaknesses or making them relevant*
Threats (T)	■ **ST Strategies** *Use strengths to avoid threats*	■ **WT Strategies** *Minimize weaknesses and avoid threats*

Listing the SWOT is not as easy as it seems. However, the second step of the SWOT analysis is even more difficult: what actions should your company take based on its strengths, weaknesses, opportunities and threats? Should you focus on using the company's strengths to capitalize on opportunities, or acquire strengths in order to be able to capture opportunities? Or should you actively try to minimize weaknesses and avoid threats?

'SO' and 'WT' strategies are quite obvious. A company should do what it is good at when the opportunity arises and steer clear of businesses that it does not have the competencies for. Less obvious and much more daring are 'WO' strategies. When a company decides to take on an opportunity despite not possessing the requisite strengths, it must either:

- develop the required strengths
- buy or borrow the required strengths
- outmanoeuvre the competition.

Companies that use 'ST' strategies essentially 'buy or bust' their way out of trouble. This happens when big players fend off smaller ones by means of expensive price wars, insurmountable marketing budgets, multiple channel promotions, etc. Some companies use *scenario planning* to try and anticipate and thus be prepared for this type of future threat.

The final analysis

The value of a SWOT analysis lies mainly in the fact that it constitutes a self-assessment for management. The problem, however, is that elements (SWOT) appear deceptively simple. Actually deciding what the strengths and weaknesses of your organization are, as well as assessing the impact and probability of opportunities and threats, is far more complex than at first sight. Furthermore, beyond classification of the SWOT elements, the model offers no assistance with the tricky task of translating them into strategic alternatives. The inherent risk of making incorrect assumptions when assessing the SWOT elements often causes management to dither when it comes to choosing between various strategic alternatives, frequently resulting in unnecessary and/or undesirable delays.

Value-based management

The big idea

Value-based management (VBM) is an integrated management approach aiming for maximization of shareholder value. The approach entails planning, assessment, compensation and organizational communication related to rewarding for performance based on shareholder value added. VBM has gained popularity in recent years, as corporate governance has become a hot issue and shareholders come from more and more segments of the population. The mere survival of a corporation increasingly depends on its ability to create value.

There seem to be three essential areas of discussion in value-based management:

1. Different value metrics:

   – what is value?

2. What influence do managers – at different levels – have on it?

   – Is it understandable?

   – Is it controllable?

   – Can it be manipulated?

   In other words, is it fair?

3. To what extent should compensation be directly linked to value creation?

With regard to the first issue, there are many value-based measure acronyms:

- economic profit (EP)
- cash value added (CVA)
- net present value (NPV)

- internal rate of return (IRR)
- cash flow return on investment (CFROI)
- internal total shareholder return (iTSR)
- economic value added (EVA)
- economic earnings (EE).

It is beyond the scope of this brief description of VBM to venture into more details on the above value measures. The most important thing to understand is that different companies require different performance-based measures and compensation schemes. The end result usually signifies the compromise between fairness and simplicity.

When to use it

The first two steps in any VBM approach are understanding and determining the so-called value drivers. This can be done in a top-down approach. Examples of value drivers are sales turnover, margins, capital structure ratios, working capital ratios, etc.

How to quantify value drivers and link them measurably in an integrated manner, i.e. to functional responsibilities for which teams and/or individuals can be held responsible, is a third, much more difficult step. When executives and particularly managers lack direct control over one

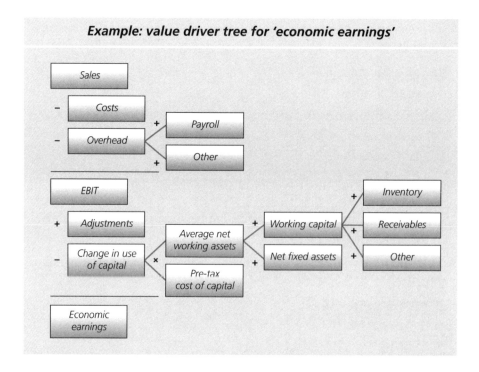

Example: value driver tree for 'economic earnings'

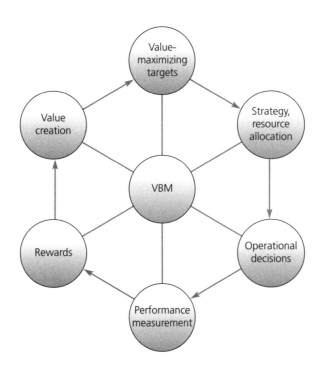

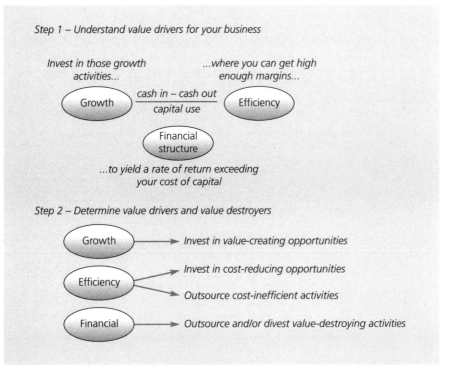

key measure of value, namely the stock price, this gets tricky. Value drivers should therefore be determined for each managerial level.

The fourth step is organizing rights and accountability over areas of functional responsibility. This requires not only accounting adjustments or perhaps a third set of books, it might in fact result in a complete reorganization. Without a doubt, this is when the company needs to be fully committed to VBM.

The final analysis

VBM is not just a financial scorecard for the organization. It is meant to generate an ongoing awareness of value in every management decision over the use of resources. VBM should cause a fundamental change in thinking about growth, profits, and budgets.

Traditional (external) accounting and (internal) budgeting methods are insufficient for successful application of VBM concepts.

VBM requires full commitment and high priority from the board, executives and management of a company in order to succeed.

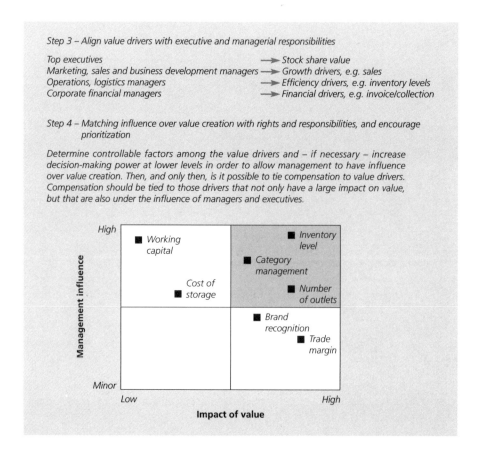

Step 3 – Align value drivers with executive and managerial responsibilities

Top executives	⟶ Stock share value
Marketing, sales and business development managers	⟶ Growth drivers, e.g. sales
Operations, logistics managers	⟶ Efficiency drivers, e.g. inventory levels
Corporate financial managers	⟶ Financial drivers, e.g. invoice/collection

Step 4 – Matching influence over value creation with rights and responsibilities, and encourage prioritization

Determine controllable factors among the value drivers and – if necessary – increase decision-making power at lower levels in order to allow management to have influence over value creation. Then, and only then, is it possible to tie compensation to value drivers. Compensation should be tied to those drivers that not only have a large impact on value, but that are also under the influence of managers and executives.

The value chain

The big idea

Competitive advantage, argues Michael Porter (1985), can be understood only by looking at a firm as a whole. Cost advantages and successful differentiation are found in the chain of activities that a firm performs to deliver value to its customers.

Advantage or disadvantage can occur at any one of five primary and four secondary activities. Together, these activities form the value chain for every firm.

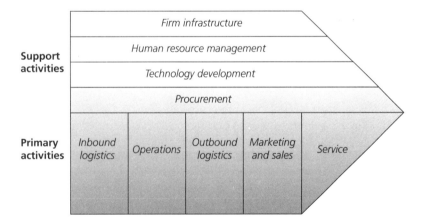

Inbound logistics activities are activities such as receiving, storing, listing, grouping inputs to the product. Included are functions such as materials handling, warehousing, inventory management, transportation scheduling and managing suppliers.

Operations include machining, packaging, assembly, maintenance of equipment, testing, operational management, etc.

Outbound logistics refers to such activities as order processing, warehousing, scheduling transportation and distribution management.

Marketing and sales are all activities that make or convince buyers to purchase the company's products. Included are: advertising, promotion, selling, pricing, channel selection, retail management, etc.

Service is to do with maintaining the product after sale, thus guaranteeing quality and/or adding value in other ways, such as installation, training, servicing, providing spare parts and upgrading. Service enhances the product value and also allows for after-sale (commercial) interaction with the buyer.

Porter refers to **procurement** as a secondary activity, although many purchasing gurus would argue that it is (at least partly) a primary activity. Included are such activities as purchasing raw materials, servicing, supplies, negotiating contracts with suppliers, securing building leases and so on.

With **technology development,** Porter refers to such activities as R&D, product and/or process improvements, (re)design, developing new services, etc.

Human resource management includes recruitment and education, as well as compensation, employee retention and other means to fully capitalise on human resources.

The **firm's infrastructure**, such as general management, planning procedures, finance, accounting, public affairs and quality management, can make the difference between success and – despite the best intentions in the world – failure.

When to use it

In order to analyse the (lack of) competitive advantage, Porter suggests using the value chain to separate the company's activities in the value chain into detailed discrete activities. When broken down to a sufficient level of detail, the relative performance of your company can be determined.

The purpose of disaggregation is to help choose a generic strategy and determine areas of competitive advantage. As competitive forces are unique to industries and companies, so too are areas of competitive advantage that a company may have or need to develop.

The final analysis

Since Porter introduced his value chain in the mid-1980s, strategic planners and consultants used it extensively to map out a company's strengths and shortcomings. In analysing strategic alliances and M&A deals, the value chain is often used to get a quick overview of the possible match: one company is strong in logistics, the other in sales and service, together they would make an agile, highly commercial competitor.

Measuring or rating competitive strengths is difficult. Especially when trying to map the entire value chain and apply quantitative measurements or ratings, many companies find themselves employing large number of strategic analysts, planners and consultants.

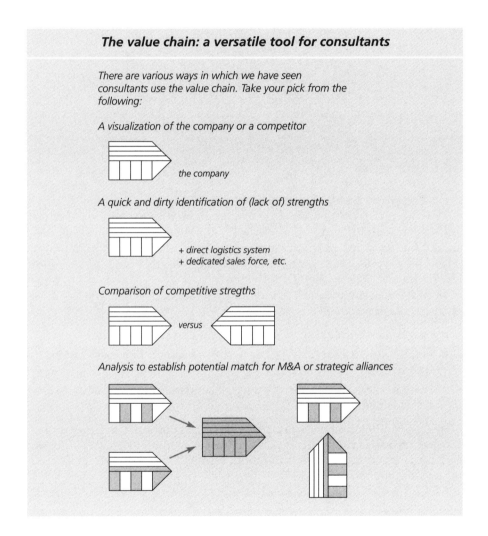

The value chain: a versatile tool for consultants

There are various ways in which we have seen consultants use the value chain. Take your pick from the following:

A visualization of the company or a competitor

the company

A quick and dirty identification of (lack of) strengths

+ direct logistics system
+ dedicated sales force, etc.

Comparison of competitive stregths

versus

Analysis to establish potential match for M&A or strategic alliances

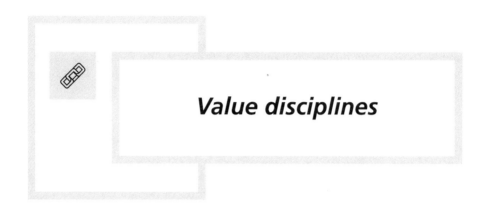

Value disciplines

The big idea

No company can be all things to all people. The key issues upon which a company will fail or succeed in delivering unique value can be identified and discussed with the value disciplines model. Every good business should have a value proposition, an operating model and a value discipline. The value discipline, if chosen deliberately and acted upon vigorously can produce significant value.

In essence, argue creators Treacy and Wiersema (1996), there are three generic value disciplines:

- operational excellence: in pursuit of the best cost position;
- product leadership: to offer the best product and moreover be the first to do so;
- customer intimacy: to be the most dependable and responsive to the needs of the customer.

Although combinations of the three value disciplines are not impossible, they can give rise to conflict. So-called hybrid models are often confusing and cause energy to be employed ineffectively. It is therefore imperative to choose – but choose carefully!

The three value disciplines can be most easily explained by looking at some examples:

Operational excellence is displayed by such companies as Wal-Mart, FedEx, Hertz, Southwest Airlines, Toyota. These companies offer relatively high quality at a relatively low price. They tend not to think up the new products or service. Instead, they observe the market's direction and execute superbly those activities known to be critical success factors. The focus is on efficiency, streamlining, supply chain integration, low inventories, no-frills, take-it-or-leave-it, managing volume dynamics.

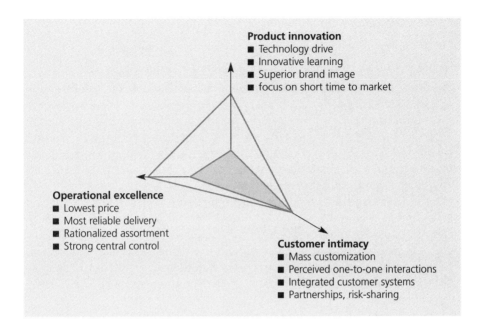

Product innovation
- Technology drive
- Innovative learning
- Superior brand image
- focus on short time to market

Operational excellence
- Lowest price
- Most reliable delivery
- Rationalized assortment
- Strong central control

Customer intimacy
- Mass customization
- Perceived one-to-one interactions
- Integrated customer systems
- Partnerships, risk-sharing

Product leaders are inventors and brand marketers such as 3M, Philips, Intel, Nike and Honda. They constantly experiment with new products, services and experiences. Their markets are either unknown or highly dynamic. Margins are sky-high, simply because of the high risk. The focus must therefore be on development, design, time-to-market, deadlines and hoping to score a few big hits to make up for countless failures.

Customer intimates will do anything to make you a satisfied customer, as long as they believe that you're worth it. The Four Seasons hotel, Marshall Field's and – yes – any good consulting firm. These companies don't believe in one-time transactions. They invest time and money in their customers. They want to know everything about their customers and work together with customers. The focus is on customer relationships (see Customer marketing and relationship management earlier in this book), exceeding expectations, customer retention, lifetime value, reliability, delegation of power to employees working with customers and 'always being nice'.

When to use it

Choosing (carefully) entails three rounds of deliberation:

1. understanding the current situation
2. discussing ideas and options
3. assessing the options, ultimately resulting in a choice being made.

In round one, senior management agrees upon the following:

- What sort of value means the most to our customers?
- How many customers focus on each type of value?
- Are there any competitors that do a better job in this respect?
- Where do we stand competitively?
- Why are we better or worse?

The second round requires senior management to determine what the three value disciplines would mean for their business, including any major changes that might be called for.

In the third round, élite groups of high-performers are instructed and guided by the moderators (usually consultants) of the first two rounds to flesh out each of the options. Internal high-performers are involved for two reasons: such activities place too high a demand on executive agendas; the people you really want to stay are able to (feel that they can) influence the future of the company, thereby gaining support. Finally, the groups present:

- operating models with design specifications for primary processes, systems, structure, etc.;
- value drivers in the model;
- the anticipated level of achievement/threshold value on the other value dimensions, despite the focus;
- potential revenues and profits (tricky!);
- financial feasibility: cost, benefits and risks;
- key success factors and pitfalls;
- transition plan for the next 2–3 years.

After the third round, a decision must be made by senior management.

The final analysis

The high level of senior management involvement in the first two rounds places a great deal of strain on the executive agenda. It is unlikely to be successful unless there is some 'warmth' for change (see Change quadrants earlier in this book). Timely involvement of the lower echelons in the strategic process of reshaping the very nature of the company they work for is also crucial: miscommunication, the perceived destruction of 'pet' products and the drawing up of abstract plans for fear of hard targets can be counterproductive if not downright destructive.

One might raise the question as to whether some companies have a choice. Any business-to-business service provider is likely to end up with operational excellence. So is any wholesaler. High-tech companies are likely to be product leaders, otherwise they wouldn't be in business. Also, changing a multi-billion, globally operating company away from focus on efficiency when the stock market plunges seems an unlikely course of action.

The three value disciplines do not by any means capture all strategic options. For instance, corporate strategic decisions, such as 'build or buy' and corporate versus product branding are not covered by the model. We therefore recommend that it be used in combination with other strategic tools.

It is difficult to choose. Not because senior management would not like to focus, but because they may need to relinquish certain values, some of which may have played an important role in getting them to their current position. Perhaps these values constitute a larger part of the stock price than can be compensated by the new focus in the short term. And last, but not least, why take the risk? Treacy and Wiersema, however, argue that the biggest risk of all lies in not choosing.

References and further reading

Activity-based costing
Kaplan, R.S. and Cooper, R. (1998) *Cost and Effect: Using Integrated Cost Systems to Drive Profitability and Performance*. Boston: Harvard Business School Press

Adizes' PAEI management roles
Adizes, I. (1979) *How to Solve Mismanagement crisis*. Homewood: Dow Jones-Irwin
Adizes, I. (1981) *Mismanagement: signaleren en oplossen*. Alphen a/d Rijn: Samsom

Ansoff's product/market grid
Ansoff, I. (1987) *Corporate Strategy* (revised edition). London: Penguin Books

The balanced scorecard
Kaplan, R.S. and. Norton, D.P (1993) 'Putting the Balanced Scorecard to Work', *Harvard Business Review*, 71, no. 5, September–October

The BCG matrix
Henderson, B.D. (1979) *Henderson on Corporate Strategy*. Cambridge: Abt Books

Belbin's team roles
Belbin, R.M. (1985) *Management Teams: Why They Succeed or Fail*. London: Heinemann

Benchmarking
Watson, G.H. (1993) *Strategic Benchmarking: How to Rate Your Company's Perfomance against the World's Best*. New York: John Wiley & Sons

The Berenschot project management model
Spall, M. van (1998) *Berenschot White Paper*

Business process redesign
Hammer, M. and Champy, J. (1993) *Reengineering the Corporation: A Manifesto for Business Revolution*. New York: Harper Business

The capability maturity model
Weber, C.V., Paulk, M.C. Wise, C.J. and Withey, J.W. (1991) *Key Practices of the Capability Maturity Model*. Technical Report CMU/SEI-91-TR-025. Pittsburgh: Software Engineering Institute

Change quadrants
The Change Factory (1999) *Het idee verandering*. Amsterdam: Uitgeverij Nieuwezijds

The chaos model
Zuijderhoudt, R.W.L. (1990) 'Chaos and the Dynamics of Self-Organization', *Human Systems Management*, 9, pp. 225–238

Zuijderhoudt R.W.L (1992) 'Principles of Synergy and Self Organization: Introduction of the Chaos Theory in Applied Organizational Science' (Dutch: 'Principes van synergie en zelfordening: introductie van de chaostheorie binnen de organisatiekunde'). *Management en Organisatie*, 46, no. 1, (January/February), pp. 15–40.

Zuijderhoudt, R.W.L., Wobben, J.J., ten Have, S. and. Busato, V. (2001) *The Logic of Chaos in Change Processes: Insights from the Chaos and Complexity Theory Applied to Change Processes in Organizations* (Dutch: *De logica van chaos in veranderingsprocessen: Inzichten uit de chaos- en complexiteitstheorie toegepast op veranderingsprocessen in organisaties*). Utrecht: Berenschot White Paper D-4795

Competing values of organizational effectiveness
Cameron, K.S. and Quinn, R. (1999) *Diagnosing and Changing Organizational Culture: Based on the Competing Values Framework*. Reading: Addison-Wesley

Quinn, R.E. and Rohrbaugh (1983) A Spatial Model of effectiveness criteria towards a competing values approach to organizational analysis, *Management Science*, 29, no. 1, pp. 363–77

Competitive analysis: Porter's five forces
Porter, M.E. (1998) *Competitive Strategy: Techniques for Analyzing Industries and Competitors*. New York: Free Press

Compliance typology
Etzioni, A. (1965) *A Comparative Analysis of Complex Organizations. On power, involvement, and their Correlates*. New York: Free Press

Drummond, H. (1993) *Power and Involvement in Organizations: An Empirical Examination of Etzioni's Compliance Theory*. Aldershot; Brookfield, USA: Avebury

Core Competencies
Hamel, G. and Prahalad, C.K. (1994) *Breakthrough Strategies for Seizing Control of Your Industry and Creating the Markets of Tomorrow*. Boston, MA: Harvard Business School Press

Hamel, G. and Prahalad, C.K. (1995) *De strijd om de toekomst: baanbrekende strategieën voor marktleiderschap en het creëren van nieuwe markten*. Schiedam: Scriptum

Hamel, G. and Prahalad, C.K. (1994) *Competing for the future*. Boston: Harvard Business School Press

Core quadrants
Offman, D.D. (1992, 2001) *Inspiration and Quality in Organizations* (Dutch: *Bezieling en kwaliteit in organisaties*), 12th edn. Utrecht, Antwerpen: Kosmos-Z&K

Covey's seven habits of highly effective people
Covey, S.R. (1999) *The 7 Habits of Highly Effective People*. London: Simon and Schuster

Customer marketing and relationship management
Kotler, P. and B. Dubois (2000) *Marketing Management: Analysis, Planning, Implementations, and Control*. Upper Saddle River, NJ: Prentice-Hall

The Deming cycle
Walton, M. and Deming, W.E. (1986) *The Deming Management Method*. New York: Dodd

The EFQM model
Hardjono, T.W., Have, S. ten and Have, W.D. ten (1996) *The European Way to Excellence: How 35 European Manufacturing, Public and Service Organizations Make Use of Quality Management*. DGIII Industry, European Commission
Hardjono, T.W. and. Hes, F.W (1994) *De Nederlandse kwaliteitsprijs en – onderscheiding*. Deventer: Kluwer Bedrijfsinformatie

Eisenhower's effective time management
Covey, S.R (1999) *The 7 Habits of Highly Effective People*. London: Simon and Schuster
— (1994) 'Met Eisenhower en Emmentaler de stress te lijf,' *Management Team*, no. 31, oktober

EVA – economic value added
Stern, J.M. and Shiely, J.S. (2001) *The EVA Challenge: Implementing Value Added Change in an Organization*. New York: John Wiley & Sons

The fifth discipline
Senge, P.M. *et al*. (1994) *The Fifth Discipline Fieldbook: Strategies and Tools for Building a Learning Organizaion*. New York: Currency
Senge, P. M. (1999) The Dance of Change: the Challenges of Sustaining Momentum in Learning Organizations. New York: Currency/Doubleday

Four competencies of the learning organization
Sprenger, C. and Have, S. ten (1996) *'Kennismanagement als moter van de lerende organisatie'*, *Holland Management Review*, Sept–Oct, pp. 73–89

Generic competitive strategies

Porter, M.E. (1980) *Competitive Strategy.* New York: Free Press

Porter, M.E. (1979) 'How Competitive Forces Shape Strategy,' *Harvard Business Review*, March, p. 137

Mintzberg, H. (1994) 'The fall and rise of strategic planning', *Harvard Business Review*, 72, no. 1, pp. 107–14

The gods of management

Handy, C. (1978–1995) *Gods of Management, the Changing Work of Organizations.* New York, Oxford: Oxford University Press

Greiner's growth model

Greiner, L.E. (1998) 'Evolution and Revolution as Organizations Grow,' *Harvard Business Review*, 76, no. 3, pp. 55–68

Hofstede's cultural dimensions

Hofstede, G. (1981) 'Culture and Organizations,' *International Studies of Management and Organization*, 10/4, pp. 15–41

Just-in-time

Monden, Y. (1998) *Toyota Production System: An Integrated Approach to Just-in-Time.* Norcross: Engineering and Management Press

Monden, Y. (1986) *Applying Just in Time: The American–Japanese Experience.* Norcross: Industrial Engineering and Management Press

Vaan, M.J.M. de (1988) *Just-in-time: strategie voor flexibiliteit en klantgerichte presentatie.* Deventer: Kluwer Bedrijfswetenschappen.

Kaizen

Imai, M. (1994) *Kaizen: The key to Japan's Competitive Succes.* New York: Random House Business Divison

Kay's distinctive capabilities

Kay, J. (1993) *Foundations of Corporate Success: How Business Strategies Add Value.* Oxford University Press

Kotter's eight phases of change

Kotter, J.P. (1990) *A Force for Change: How Leadership Differs from Management.* New York: Free Press

Kraljic's purchasing model

Kraljic. P. (1983) 'Purchasing Must Become Supply Management,' *Harvard Business Review*, September/October, pp. 109–118

Levers of control

Simons, R. (1995) *Levers of Control: How Managers Use Innovative Control Systems to Drive Strategic Renewal.* Boston MA: Harvard Business School Press

MABA analyis

Leeflang, P.S.H. (1994) *Probleemgebied Marketing.* Houten: Stenfert Kroese

The Malcolm Baldrige Award
Heaphy, M.S. and Gruska, G.F. (1995) *The Malcom Baldridge National Quality Award: A Yardstick for Quality Growth*. Reading: Addison-Wesley

Mills Steeples, M. (1992) *The Corporate Guide to the Malcom Baldrige National Quality Award: Proven Strategies for Building Quality into Your Organization*. Milwaukee: ASQC Quality Press

The marketing mix
Kotler, P. and Armstrong, G. (2001) *Principles of Marketing*. Upper Saddle River, NJ: Prentice-Hall

Maslow
Goble, F.C. (1970) *The Third Force: The Psychology of Abraham Maslow*. New York: Grossman

The 7-S framework
Pascale, R.T. and Athos, A. (1981) *The Art of Japanese Management: Applications for American Executives*. New York: Simon and Schuster

Pascale, R.T. (1990) *Managing on the Edge, How Successful Companies Use Conflict to Stay Ahead*. New York: Simon and Schuster

Mintzberg's configurations
Mintzberg, H. (1983) *Structure in Fives: Designing Effective Organizations*. Englewood Cliffs, NJ: Prentice Hall

Mintzberg. H. (1990) *Mintzberg on Management: Inside Our Strange World of Organizations*. New York: The Free Press

Mintzberg's management roles
Mintzberg. H. (1990) *Mintzberg on Management : Inside Our Strange World of Organizations*. New York: The Free Press

Mintzberg, H. (1983) *Structure in Fives: Designing Effective Organizations*. Englewood Cliffs, NJ: Prentice Hall

The neurotic organization
Kets de Vries, M. F. R. and Miller, D. (1984) *The Neurotic Organization, Diagnosing and Changing Counterproductive Styles of Management*. San Francisco, London: Jossey-Bass

Nolan's IT growth stages
Nolan, R.L. (1979) 'Managing the Crises in Data Processing,' *Harvard Business Review*, 57, no. 2 (March), pp. 115–126

Nolan, R.L. and Koot, W.J.D. (1992) 'De actualiteit van de Nolan-fasen-theorie', *Holland Management Review*, 9, no. 31, pp. 77–88

Overhead value analysis
Huys, G. (1994) *Management accounting in de praktijk*. Den Haag: SIM

Parenting advantage

Goold, M., Campbell, A. and Alexander, M. (1994) *Corporate-Level Strategy: Creating Value in the Multibusiness Company*. New York: John Wiley & Sons

The purposive change model

Bower, J.L. (2000) 'The Purpose of Change, A Commentary on Jensen and Senge' in: Beer, M. and Nohrina, N. *Breaking the Code of Change*. Boston, MA: Harvard Business School Press, pp. 83–95

Have, S. ten (2002) V*oorbeeldig veranderen: een kwestie van organiseren, proefschrift*. Twente University. Amsterdam: Uitgeverij Nieuwezijds

Risk reward analysis

Abell, H. (1998) *Risk Reward: The Art and Science of Successful Trading*. Chicago: Dearborn Financial Publishing

Scenario planning (Shell)

Ringland, G.A. (1998) *Scenario Planning: Managing for the Future*. Chichester: John Wiley & Sons

Wack, P. (1985a) 'Scenarios: Unchartered Waters Ahead', September–October

Wack, P. (1985b) 'Scenarios: Shooting the Rapids', November–December

Schools of strategy synthesis

Volberda, H.W. and Elfring, T. (2001) *Rethinking Strategy*. London: Sage

The seven forces model

Kleinendorst, B., Swieringa, H., Merkx, M. and Sprenger, C. (1988) 'Management of Cultural Change, (Dutch: 'Management van cultuurverandering'), *Elan*, 3, no. 12.

Claus, W.J. (1991, 1994) *Changing Organizational Culture: The Forces Model* (Dutch: V*eranderen van organisatieculturen: het krachtenmodel*). Schiedam: Scriptum Management

Have, S. ten (1996) *TQM and Cultural Change: A Model* (Dutch: *TQM en cultuurverandering: een model*). Sigma 1996–1

Sociotechnical organization

Sitter, L.U. de (1989) 'Moderne sociotechniek', *Gedrag en organisatie*, 2, no. 2

SWOT analysis

Hunger, J.D. and Wheelen, T.L. (1998) *Strategic Management*. Reading: Addison-Wesly

Value-based management

Copeland, T., Koller, T. and Murrin, J. (1990–2000) *Valuation: Measuring and Managing the Value of Companies*, 3rd edn. New York: John Wiley & Sons

Rappaport, A. (1986, 1998) *Creating Shareholder Value, A Guide for Managers and Investors, Revised and Updated*, 2nd edn. New York: The Free Press

The value chain

Normann, R. and Ramirez, R. (1994) *Designing Interactive Strategy: From Value Chain to Value Constellation*. Chichester: John Wiley & Sons

—— (1999) Harvard Business Review on Managing the Value Chain. HBS Press Book

Value disciplines

Treacy, M. and Wiersema, F. (1996). Discipline of Market Leaders: *Choose Your Customers, Narrow Your Focus, Dominate Your Market*. London: HarperCollins

Categorization of models

	Strategy	Organization	Primary process	Functional processes	People and behaviour
Activity-based costing				X	
Adizes' PAEI management roles		X			X
Ansoff's product/market grid	X				
The balanced scorecard		X			
The BCG matrix	X				
Belbin's team roles					X
Benchmarking			X	X	
The Berenschot project management model				X	
Business process redesign		X			
The capability maturity model				X	
Change quadrants		X			X
The chaos model		X			X
Competing values of organizational effectiveness	X	X			
Competitive analysis: Porter's five forces	X				
Compliance typology					X
Core competencies	X				
Core quadrants					X
Covey's seven habits of highly effective people					X
Customer marketing and relationship management				X	
The Deming cycle		X			
The EFQM model		X			
Eisenhower's effective time management					X

	Strategy	Organization	Primary process	Functional processes	People and pehaviour
EVA – economic value added				X	
The fifth discipline					X
Four competencies of the learning organization		X			
Generic competitive strategies	X				
The gods of management					X
Greiner's growth model		X			
Hofstede's cultural dimensions					X
Just-in-time			X		
Kaizen		X	X		
Kay's distinctive capabilities	X				
Kotter's eight phases of change		X			X
Kraljic's purchasing model				X	
Levers of control		X			
MABA analysis	X				
The Malcolm Baldridge Award		X			
The marketing mix				X	
Maslow					X
The 7-S framework		X			
Mintzberg's configurations		X			
Mintzberg's management roles					X
The neurotic organization					X
Nolan's IT growth stages				X	
Overhead value analysis				X	
Parenting advantage		X			
The purposive change model		X			X
Risk reward analysis				X	
Scenario planning (Shell)	X				
Schools of strategy synthesis	X				
The seven forces model		X			X
Sociotechnical organization					X
SWOT Analysis	X				
Value-based management		X		X	
The value chain	X	X			
Value disciplines				X	

Index

control
IT growth stage 156, 157
levers of 119–22
control crisis 94, 96
co-ordinating mechanisms 144
co-ordination phase 94, 96–7
co-ordinator role 18, 19
core competencies 52–5
core quadrants 56–8
core quality 56, 57
corporate development 163
corporate life cycle 7
cost leadership strategy 86–7, 88
cost objects 3
costing, activity-based (ABC) 2–4, 161
Covey's seven habits model 59–61
creativity phase 94, 95
crises 94, 95–7
culture
cultural dimensions 98–100
organizational 36, 90–3
customer focus 127, 128, 129
customer intimacy 196–7
customer marketing 62–5
customer perspective 13
customer pyramid 62–4, 65
customer relationship management
62–5

data processing (DP) growth 156–8
decentralization 144, 145
decisional roles 148
deconcentration 156, 157
defined level 32, 33
delegation phase 94, 96
Deming cycle 27, 66–7
depressive neurosis 150, 151
design see organization design
diagnostic control systems 120, 121
differentiation strategy 86–7, 88
diffusion 81, 83, 85
Dionysus 90, 91
direct supervision 144
direction
Greiner's growth model 94, 95–6
purposive change model 166–7, 168
disseminator role 148
distinctive capabilities 108–11
distribution (place) 133
disturbance handler role 148
diversification 9, 10

diversified organization 142, 144
dogs 16
dramatic neurosis 150, 151
dynamic capability school 176, 177
dysfunctions, organizational 150–5

economic earnings (EE) 190
economic value added (EVA) 74–6
effectiveness
highly effective people's habits 59–61
organizational 41–3
time management 72–3
eight phases of change model 112–14
80/20 rule 63, 64
Eisenhower's effective time
management model 72–3
elimination of muda (waste) 105, 106
empathy 155
empowerment 36
enablers (organizational areas) 68–70
entrepreneur (E) role 5, 6, 8, 148
entrepreneurial organization 142,
144, 146
European Foundation for Quality
Management (EFQM) model
68–71
existential culture 90, 91
existing competitors 46, 47
expansion phase 156, 157
expert power 51
exploitation 81, 83, 85
external focus 41–2
external orientation 7, 8

feedback 166–7, 168
femininity vs masculinity dimension
98, 99, 100
fifth discipline model 77–80
figurehead role 148
financial impact/risk 115, 116, 117
financial perspective 12–13
finisher role 18, 19, 20
firm infrastructure 193, 194
five Cs of the individual change
process 154
five forces model 44–7
five Ss 106
flexibility 41–2
focus strategy 86, 87
foresight 53

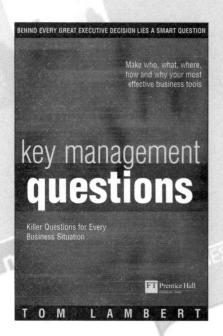